Geography Matters 1

HIGHER

Series Editor:

John Hopkin

Authors:

Nicola Arber with Jill Sim and Rachel McCarthy, Bournville School, Birmingham

Sue Lomas, Henbury High School, Macclesfield

Garrett Nagle, St Edward's School, Oxford

Linda Thompson, Sandbach School, Sandbach

Paul Thompson, Ounsdale High School, Wolverhampton

666339

Heinemann Educational Publishers
Halley Court, Jordan Hill, Oxford, OX2 8EJ
part of Harcourt Education

Heinemann is the registered trademark of Harcourt Education Limited.

© Nicola Arber, Sue Lomas, Garrett Nagle, Linda Thompson, Paul Thompson, 2001

First published in 2001

04 03 02
10 9 8 7

British Library Cataloguing in Publication Data
A catalogue record for this book is available from the British Library

ISBN 0 435 355074

Designed and illustrated by Gecko Ltd, Bicester, Oxon, Dave Mostyn and Peter Bull
Original illustrations © Heinemann Educational Publishers 2000
Printed and bound in the UK by Bath Colourbooks ,

Acknowledgements
The authors and publishers would like to thank the following for permission to use copyright material:

Maps and extracts
p.6, 7 Philips Foundation Atlas 7th Edition / George Philip Ltd; p.13 Maps reproduced from Ordnance Survey maps with the permission of the Controller of Her Majesty's Stationery Office © Crown Copyright; License No. 398020; p.14, 16 McDonalds; p.26 Encarta / Microsoft Corporation; p.30 Key Geography Interactions / Stanley Thornes; p.30 Kandilli Observatory, Istanbul; p.33 Angela Topping, After the Earthquake, first published in Can You Hear? Poems / Oxfam, Pan Macmillan 1992. Reproduced by permission of Oxfam GB; p.34 National Earthquake Information Centre; p.37 Earthquake Engineering Research Institute; p.41 SITREP 16, 13th March 2000 / UNICEF; p.51 UK Census Bureau; p.56 Philips Foundation Atlas 7th Edition / George Philip Ltd; p.62, 63, 64, 65, 66 Maps reproduced from Ordnance Survey maps with the permission of the Controller of Her Majesty's Stationery Office © Crown Copyright; License No. 398020; p.79 The Sunday Telegraph, 1st November 1998; p.83 Easter 1998 Flood report, Volume 1 / Environmental Agency; p.84, 86 www.guardianunlimited.co.uk / The Guardian; p.85 The Guardian 4th March, 10th March 2000, 28th March 2000; p.86 The Daily Telegraph 29th March 2000; p.94 Philips Foundation Atlas 7th Edition / George Philip Ltd; p.96 The Met Office; p.101, 106 The Football Association Premier League National Fan Survey 1998/99; p.105 London Transport Museum; p.105 Chiltern Railways; p.108, 111, 112 Maps reproduced from Ordnance Survey maps with the permission of the Controller of Her Majesty's Stationery Office © Crown Copyright; License No. 398020; p.109 Aston Local Plan / Department of Planning, Birmingham City Council; p.114 Philips Foundation Atlas 7th Edition / George Philip Ltd.

Photographs
Cover photos by Tony Stone and PA News.
4 A Corbis / Craig Aurness; 4 B Corbis / Yann Arthus-Bertrand; 4 C Corbis / Catherine Karnow; 4 D Gettyone Stone; 4 E Corbis / Galen Rowell; 4 F The Stock Market; 5 G Corbis / Paul A.Souders; 5 H Corbis / Vince Streano; 6 SPL/NRSC Ltd; 8 A SPL/Tom Van Sant/ Geosphere Project/Planetary Visions; 10 A Dave Marriott – Wimpy; 14 F Corbis / Owen Franken; 20 A Associated Press; 20 B Corbis / AFP; 20 C Corbis / Nik Wheeler; 20 D Associated Press; 20 E Corbis / AFP; 21 F; Associated Press; 21 G Corbis / George Hall; 21 H Associated Press; 21 I Rex Features / Sipa Press; 21 J Rex Features / Sipa Press; 25 A GeoScience Features Picture Library; 27 C Corbis / Bettmann; 27 D Rex Features / Sipa Press; 27 E R.P.Hoblitt, US Geological Survey; 28 F Rex Features / Sipa Press; 28 G Corbis / Yann Arthus-Bertrand; 28 H Rex Features / Sipa Press; 28 K Rex Features / Sipa Press; 29 L Tokai University Research & Information Center (TRIC); 29 M Corbis /Paul A. Souders; 32 A Rex Features / Sipa Press, 32 B Rex Features / Sipa Press; 32 E Associated Press; 32 F Associated Press; 32 D Corbis / AFP; 32 C Corbis / Joseph Sohm; 33 Rex Features / Sipa Press; 34 D Rex Features / Sipa Press; 35 E Rex Features / Sipa Press; 36 K Corbis / AFP; 36 J Rex Features / Sipa Press; 36 L Rex Features / Sipa Press; 38 A Corbis / Craig Lovell; 38 B Earthquake Hazard Centre / Rajendra Desai; 38 C Camera Press; 39 F SPL/David Parker; 39 F SPL/David Parker; 37 N Corbis / AFP; 40 B U.S. Agency for International Development and the Miami-Dade Fire Rescue Squad; 42 A SPL; 42 B James Davis Worldwide; 42 C Corbis / Michael S. Yamashita; 44 A Corbis / John Noble; 47 C Eye Ubiquitous; 48 D Gettyone Stone; 49 E Corbis / Wolfgang Kaehler; 50 A The Stock Market; 52 A The Stock Market; 55 C Panos Pictures; 55 D Panos Pictures; 56 B Corbis / Morton Beebe; 56 C Still Pictures; 57 D Gettyone Stone; 57 E The Stock Market; 58 A Corbis / Charles & Josette Lenars; 58 B Corbis / Paul A. Souders; 58 C Corbis / Uwe Waiz; 59 E Gettyone Stone; 59 D SPL/Rosenfled Images Ltd; 59 F Panos Pictures; 59 G John Hopkin; 62 B Photoair; 62 D Britain on View; 63 F Photoair; 64 G Welsh Tourist Board; 65 J Welsh Tourist Board; 66 Worcester Tourist Board; 69 A Sue Cunningham / SCP; 70 C Corbis; 70 D Sue Cunningham / SCP; 71 E Sue Cunningham; 72 F Sue Cunningham; 72 G Environmental Images; 74 A Press Association; 75 B Newsteam International; 78 A Alan Bowring; 79 B Press Association; 82 A Coventry Evening Standard; 85 A Associated Press / Karel Prinsloo Stringer; 85 B Associated Press / Karel Prinsloo Stringer; 86 C Associated Press / Juda Ngwenya; 86 D Press Association; 88 B Britain on View; 88 C Gettyone Stone; 88 D Britain on View; 89 D Bubbles; 89 A Gettyone Stone; 92 H Gettyone Stone; 92 A The Stock Market; 92 B Gettyone Stone; 92 C Gettyone Stone; 92 I The Stock Market; 92 D Britain on View; 92 E The Stock Market; 92 F Tony Stone; 92 G Bluewater; 93 A Tony Stone; 93 C John Hopkin; 93 B John Hopkin; 93 D John Hopkin; 93 E John Hopkin; 97 C University of Dundee; 100 A Gettyone Stone; 100 B Garret Nagle; 100 C The Stock Market; 10 D Panos Pictures / Jeremy Homer; 103 D Popperfoto; 106 C Corbis / TempSport; 109 C Skyscan; 110 F John Hopkin; 111 B Garrett Nagle; 112 D Garret Nagle.

The publishers have made every effort to trace the copyright holders, but if they have inadvertently overlooked any, they will be pleased to make the necessary arrangements at the first opportunity.

Websites
Links to appropriate websites are given throughout the book. Although these were up to date at the time of writing, it is essential for teachers to preview these sites before using them with pupils. This will ensure that the web address (URL) is still accurate and the content is suitable for your needs.

We suggest that you bookmark useful sites and consider enabling pupils to access them through the school intranet. We are bringing this to your attention, as we are aware of legitimate sites being appropriated illegally by people wanting to distribute unsuitable or offensive material. We strongly advise you to purchase suitable screening software so that pupils are protected from unsuitable sites and their material.

If you do find that the links given no longer work, or the content is unsuitable, please let us know. Details of changes will be posted on our website.

Tel: 01865 888058 www.heinemann.co.uk

Contents

❶ Making connections   **4**

Where in the world?   6
Where are we?   8
Passport to the world   9
Enquire within   10
Review and reflect   19

❷ Restless Earth   **20**

Where do volcanoes and earthquakes occur?   22
Why do volcanoes and earthquakes occur where they do?   24
What are volcanoes?   25
What happens when a volcano erupts?   26
What happens in an earthquake?   30
How do earthquakes affect people and places?   32
How can people make earthquakes less of a hazard?   38
How can aid help the victims of earthquakes and volcanoes?   40
Why do people choose to live in active zones?   42
Review and reflect   43

❸ People everywhere   **44**

Why is the population of the world going up so much?   46
It's not just a numbers game!   50
Population density   52
Population distribution: Where do people live in Mali?   54
Distribution of population: Looking globally   56
Population: Review and Reflect   57
What is a settlement?   58
Settlement sites   60
Settlement along the River Severn   61
The living city   68
Review and reflect   73

❹ Flood disaster   **74**

What happens to water when it reaches the ground?   76
What causes the River Severn in the United Kingdom to flood?   78
What are the effects of the River Severn flooding?   80
How do people respond to flooding in the United Kingdom?   82
What caused the flooding in Mozambique?   84
The effects of the floods in Mozambique   85
Review and reflect   87

❺ Exploring England   **88**

What is England really like?   89
What do you mean by England?   90
What images do you have of England?   92
Where are you in England?   93
What is the English weather like?   94
Why does Britain's weather change?   96
Planning a tour of England   98
Review and reflect   99

❻ World sport   **100**

Soundbites on sport   101
Football - the world's favourite sport   102
Getting to a football match   104
Football - a changing industry   106
Where are football grounds located?   108
The World Cup   114
Review and reflect   115

Glossary   **116**

Index   **120**

Throughout the book these symbols are used with activities that use literacy, numeracy and ICT skills.

A An oasis in the Sahara desert, near Timbuktu

Learn about

In this unit you will learn about the connections between places in different parts of the world and how they are connected to places you know.

You will also find out how to carry out an enquiry. This is the way that geographers find out more about things they want to know. You will learn:

- how to locate places on atlas maps
- how to ask geographical questions
- how to collect and present data
- how to make conclusions.

B The River Amazon

C Bombay

D New York

E The North Pole

F St Lucia

G Sydney

H Mount Fuji, Japan

1. Choose one of the photographs **A–H**. Think of some questions you would like to ask to find out more about the place it shows. Write your questions down.

2. Compare your questions with those of a partner. Choose the four questions that you think are most important. Then prepare an **annotated** sketch of the area in your photograph like the one in **I**, answering all the questions you have asked. Use an atlas, books from the library, CD-ROMS or the Internet to gather your information. **ICT**

How to ...

... draw an annotated sketch

⑥ A sketch that is *annotated* has labels describing its main features. Sometimes these labels will explain a feature too.

Animals are adapted to the hot, dry **climate**, like the camel which has a hump to store fat and water.

People's clothes are light in colour to reflect the heat and to keep them cool.

The sky is blue with very little cloud, so the weather is very hot during the day.

There is little rainfall in this area so most of the ground is bare.

This is a natural environment.

Trees grow where there is a water supply, for example at an oasis

I An annotated sketch of an oasis

Activities

3. With your partner, look at photographs **A–H**. Put the photos into pairs by making connections between them. For example, **A** and **B** both show trees as the main type of vegetation. There is more than one correct answer – your answer is right as long as you have found a good connection.

4. Copy the table below. Write down the letters for each of your pairs with a short explanation of the connection. The first one has been done for you.

Pair	Connection
A and B	Both show trees as the main vegetation

Where in the world?

All the places in the photographs on pages 6 and 7 can be found using an **atlas**. An atlas is a book of maps which shows different physical and human features of the world.

The *contents page* of an atlas is found at the front. It contains lists of different countries or continents. It also lists maps which show other things about a country or continent, like types of farming or different climate areas – these are known as **thematic** maps. You can see a typical contents page in **A**.

The *index* at the back of the atlas will help you find a particular place. Places are listed in alphabetical order. The entry will give the page number and a grid square reference, and the latitude and longitude may also appear. The index entry for Manchester is shown in **B**, and map **D** shows an extract from an atlas that includes Manchester.

A

BRITISH ISLES SECTION

2–3	**British Isles from Space**
4–5	**England and Wales**
6	**Scotland**
7	**Ireland**
8	**British Isles:** Relief
9	**British Isles:** Counties and Regions

B

Manchester	**4**	**D3**	53°N	2°W
place or feature	*page*	*grid square*	*latitude*	*longitude*

C Satellite image of north-west England

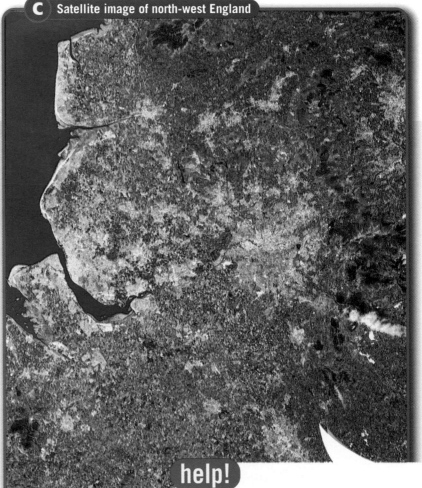

Activities

① Find each of the following features on map **D** opposite.

- **a** Liverpool
- **b** The Peak
- **c** Dee Estuary
- **d** Manchester Airport
- **e** The Pennines
- **f** Macclesfield.

② Copy the table below. Complete it for features **a–f** above. The first one has been done for you.

Feature	Grid square	Description
Liverpool	C3	City

③ **a** Write the name of the place you live in as an atlas entry.

b Choose two or more places that you know in other countries. Write out their atlas entries.

④ Use the satellite photograph **C** to find the places in question **I**.

help!

C is a true-colour photo of part of the area shown in **D**. The brown areas are hills; the pinkish-grey areas show **settlements** and the green and yellow areas show **vegetation**.

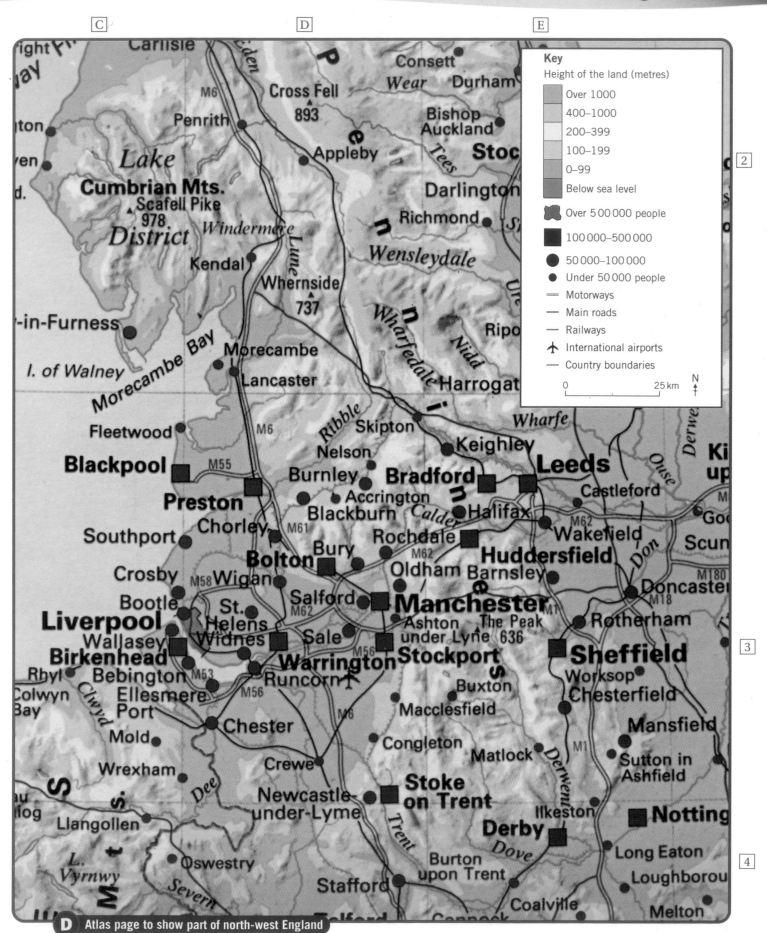

Key

Height of the land (metres)

- Over 1000
- 400–1000
- 200–399
- 100–199
- 0–99
- Below sea level

- Over 5 00 000 people
- 100 000–500 000
- 50 000–100 000
- Under 50 000 people

= Motorways
— Main roads
— Railways
✈ International airports
-- Country boundaries

0   25 km

N

D Atlas page to show part of north-west England

Where are we?

A Satellite photograph of the Earth

Figure **A** is a photograph of the world taken from a satellite. Actually, it is made up of lots of photographs taken at different times as the satellite circled the Earth, because you cannot see the whole surface of the Earth at the same time. This is because the Earth is a sphere. It is also impossible to draw an accurate map of the world on a flat surface. In the drawing of the globe below only half the world can be seen. To represent the whole Earth as in the photograph, some places will be squashed up and some stretched.

Lines of latitude are imaginary lines drawn around the Earth from east to west. The line of latitude around the centre of the Earth is called the **Equator**. Latitude is measured in degrees north (N) or south (S) of the Equator.

Lines running north to south around the Earth pass through the North and South Poles and are called **lines of longitude**. They are all the same length. The line 0° of longitude passes through Greenwich, near London, and is called the **Prime Meridian**. Lines of longitude are numbered in degrees east (E) and west (W) of the Prime Meridian (see **B**).

So that places can be found exactly, each degree of latitude and longitude is divided into 60 **minutes**. Every place has a latitude and longitude co-ordinate, for example Manchester is at 53°N 2°W.

Activity

1. Copy out the table below. It shows the latitude and longitude of some places, including those in the photographs on pages 4 and 5. Use an atlas to complete the table.

Place	Latitude	Longitude	Place	Latitude	Longitude
Timbuktu	16°N		North Pole	90°N	0°E
New York		76°W	St Lucia	14°N	
River Amazon		50°W	Venice		12°E
Bombay	18°N		Sydney		
Mount Fuji	35°N		Salt Lake City		

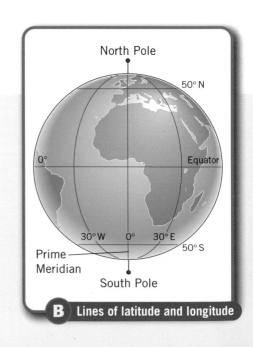

B Lines of latitude and longitude

Passport to the world

There are lots of places around the world that we have links to every day. This is a picture of Jenny sitting at home in her kitchen. The picture is labelled with some of the places she has had contacts with today.

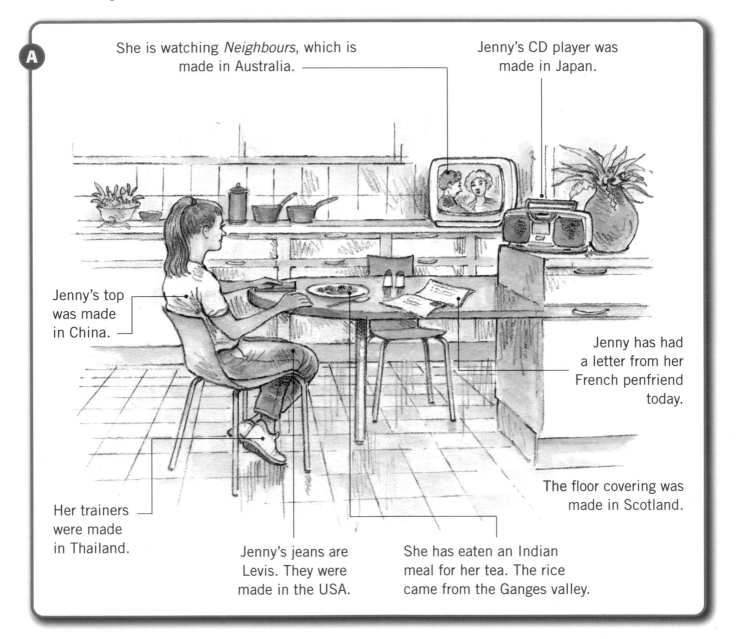

A

She is watching *Neighbours*, which is made in Australia.

Jenny's CD player was made in Japan.

Jenny's top was made in China.

Jenny has had a letter from her French penfriend today.

Her trainers were made in Thailand.

The floor covering was made in Scotland.

Jenny's jeans are Levis. They were made in the USA.

She has eaten an Indian meal for her tea. The rice came from the Ganges valley.

Activities

1. Make a list of all the places and countries which Jenny has had links with today. Mark them onto a world map. Use an atlas to help you.

2. Give your map a key and a title to include the words *linked, places, world*.

3. Make your own list of places in a world diary. Keep this diary for a month and then show all the places you have been linked to on a world map. Keep this list and the work you do with it in your World Passport.

Enquire within

The questions that geographers ask about people and places can often be answered by what they call an **enquiry** or investigation. When you carry out an enquiry there are a series of steps to follow. In the next pages you are going to learn about these steps and carry out an enquiry of your own.

Step 1: Asking questions

Geographers often carry out an enquiry to find out about a problem or issue in their local area. Sometimes they want to test a **hypothesis** (theory) or idea that they have about something. An enquiry may also be carried out to help people make a decision about something. For example, a company may have applied for planning permission to open a new fast food restaurant in your area. An enquiry question that you might like to ask is:

Why are fast food restaurants located where they are?

What sort of information do you need to help you make a decision about this?

Some questions you might like to ask include:

- ⚙ What is fast food and what are fast food restaurants like?
- ⚙ Who uses fast food restaurants and where do they come from?
- ⚙ Is there a need for more fast food restaurants in the area?
- ⚙ What effects do fast food restaurants have on the area around them?
- ⚙ What alternatives are there to providing another restaurant?

How to ...

... ask geographical questions

Nearly all geographical questions will include at least one of the words:
- ⚙ what?
- ⚙ how?
- ⚙ where?
- ⚙ who?
- ⚙ why?

If there are many things you want to ask about, you should ask several short questions.

A Inside a fast food restaurant

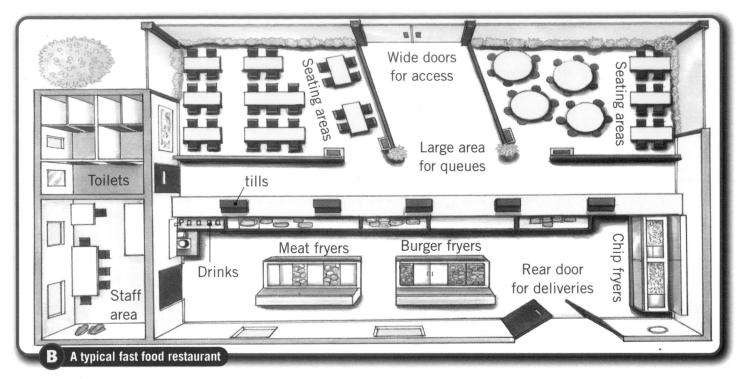

Wide doors for access

Seating areas

Seating areas

Large area for queues

Toilets

tills

Chip fryers

Meat fryers

Burger fryers

Drinks

Rear door for deliveries

Staff area

B A typical fast food restaurant

What are the features of a fast food restaurant?

The sketch in **B** above shows a typical fast food restaurant. There are several features that are common to fast food restaurants but which are not typical of other types of restaurants.

Activities

1. Copy the following table, which shows features of a fast food restaurant. Give reasons to explain why restaurants have these features. The first one has been done for you. Then add some features of your own, and explanations for them.

Description	Explanation
Food is designed to be eaten without cutlery	Saves washing up, so fewer people need to be employed
Self-service	
Open-plan restaurants	
Several serving points	
Large signs on the outside of the restaurant	
A lot of disposable wrapping material	

2. Use the ideas you have collected to make a poster advertising a fast food restaurant, pointing out the features you have mentioned in your table. Your poster should try to persuade a group of people to come and eat at your restaurant. Choose from:

- school friends

- parents with young children

- single people who live alone.

You could use the desktop publishing software on your computer.

Step 2: Collecting information

Once you have decided which questions to ask, you must decide how you are going to find the answers to them. Some questions are easy to answer straight away. For others you need to find out more detailed information, from books, from visiting places or from asking other people questions. The information geographers can collect can be divided into two types:

⑥ **Primary data** is information that you find out for yourself by looking, counting or asking people questions.

⑥ **Secondary data** is information that you collect by looking at maps or books, or by using CD-ROMS or the Internet.

Collecting primary data using a questionnaire

Suppose that you want to find out about the types of fast food restaurants that your class likes to visit. You might choose to use a questionnaire, or you might want to make a survey of what types of restaurant are available in your town. You could investigate how far it is to the restaurants from each person's home, or which type of fast food your class likes best.

How to...

... use a questionnaire

⑥ Decide on the things you want to find out about.

⑥ Try to ask questions which have answers that can be put into categories.

⑥ Give some choices for people to give as an answer.

⑥ Don't ask too many questions – people get bored!

⑥ You could use a data-handling program to help you. (ICT)

Activity

① Some students have designed questionnaire **C** about fast food.
Look at each question carefully and give a reason why the students wanted to ask it.

> **1** **Which age group do you belong to?**
>
> 0–15 ☐   16–25 ☐   26–40 ☐
> 41–60 ☐   over 60 ☐
>
> **2** **Where do you live?**   In a town/city centre ☐
> In the suburbs ☐   In the countryside ☐
>
> **3** **Do you like fast food?**   Yes ☐   No ☐
>
> **4** **If yes, what is your favourite fast food?**
>
> Burgers ☐
> Pizza ☐
> Chicken ☐
> Fish'n'chips ☐
> Other ☐   Please name _____
>
> **5** **How far away from your home is your nearest fast food restaurant?**
>
> Under 1 km ☐   1–3 km ☐   3–6 km ☐   more than 6 km ☐

C

Collecting secondary data using maps

Another way to collect information is by using maps. You could, for example, use a map to find out what types of fast food restaurants are available in your town or city. Map **D** shows the layout of a city centre.

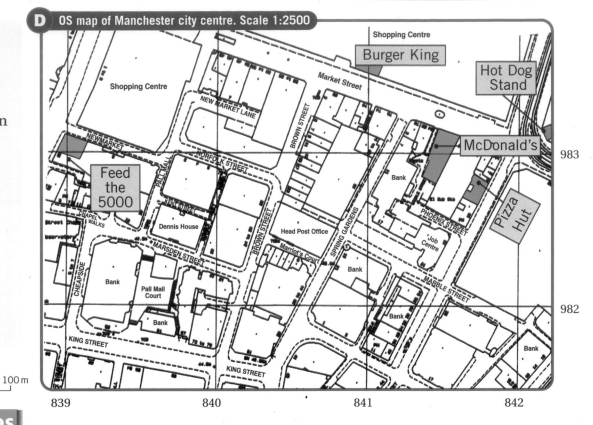

D OS map of Manchester city centre. Scale 1:2500

0   100 m

Activities

❶ On a copy of map **D**, colour in all the fast food restaurants.

❷ Imagine you have to visit all the restaurants to make a survey of their features. Work out a route that allows you to visit all of them. Draw your route onto your map.

❸ Use the scale to work out how far you will have to walk. The instructions in the How to ... box will help you. ①②③

❹ Write a description of your route to tell someone else how to follow it.

❺ What do you notice about the location of the restaurants?

How to ...

... measure distances on a map

Measure the distance you have to travel by following these instructions.

1 Take a piece of paper with a straight edge.

2 Place the straight edge between the beginning and end of your journey.

3 Mark the two points on your piece of paper.

4 Move the paper to the scale line at the edge of the map.

5 With the first point on 0, read the distance you would have to travel on the scale line.

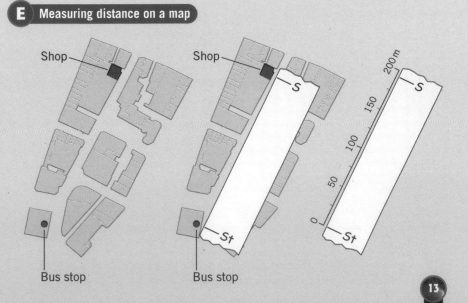

E Measuring distance on a map

Step 3: Showing your results

Once you have collected your data, you need to change it from simple written answers and numbers into graphs, maps or diagrams. These should show the information in a more interesting way and make it easier to understand.

Investigating McDonald's in Great Britain

The first McDonald's restaurant opened in the USA in 1955. McDonald's opened its first UK restaurant in London in 1974. The restaurant proved to be very popular and the company opened more and more restaurants in the London area. Then, with an increase in demand between 1980 and 1984, the restaurants spread northwards to the Birmingham and Manchester regions. Today there are over 860 restaurants throughout Great Britain. Table **G** below shows how the restaurants have spread.

F A McDonald's fast food restaurant in Paris, France

Year	London	South-east England	Midlands	East Anglia	North-west England	North-east England	South-west England	Wales	Scotland	Total
1980	47	2	0	2	0	0	0	0	0	51
1988	106	32	46	20	46	24	2	10	8	294
1998	194	120	122	61	124	73	65	32	45	836

G McDonald's restaurants in Great Britain

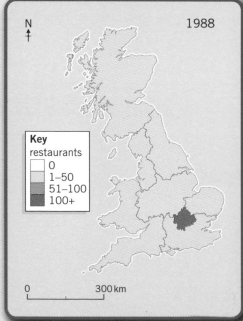

H This set of maps shows the growth of McDonald's restaurants in Great Britain since 1980

Activities

① Use the writing frame to describe the growth of McDonald's in Great Britain. 📖

② Use blank copies of a map showing the regions of Great Britain. Draw graphs to show the distribution of restaurants, using the data from table **G**. ①②③

   a Using the data for 1980, make a bar chart of the information, with a bar located in each region.

   b Using the data for 1988, make a pictogram map of the information. What symbol could you use to show the information?

   c Using the data for 1998, make a dot map of the information, following the instructions below.

③ Compare the maps and graphs you have drawn.

   a Which was the quickest to draw?

   b Which map or graph shows the information in the best way? Give reasons for your answer.

   c Can you think of any other ways you could have shown the information?

④ Compare your maps to map **I** of population distribution in Great Britain. Are there any similarities and differences between the maps?

Growth of McDonald's in Great Britain

In 1974 McDonald's opened its first restaurant in Great Britain.

By 1980 there were restaurants in _____

By 1988 there were restaurants in _____

In 1998 the number of restaurants had grown to _____ and they could be found _____

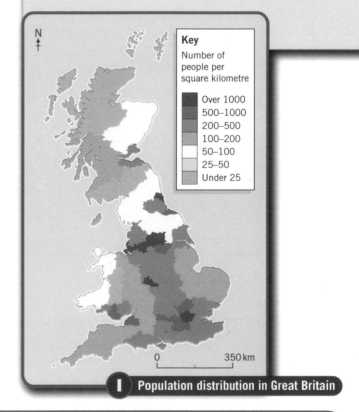

Key
Number of people per square kilometre

⬛	Over 1000
⬛	500–1000
⬛	200–500
⬛	100–200
⬜	50–100
⬛	25–50
⬛	Under 25

0   350 km

I   **Population distribution in Great Britain**

How to ...

... draw a dot distribution map

1   You are going to show the distribution of McDonald's restaurants in 1998 on a map of Great Britain by drawing dots in each region.

2   Find the number of restaurants in the region from table **G**.

3   Use one dot for every ten restaurants:

   ⑥ Divide the number of restaurants by 10.

   ⑥ Give the number to the nearest 10; for London, 194/10 = 19.4 = 19 dots.

4   Draw the dots evenly over the region on your map.

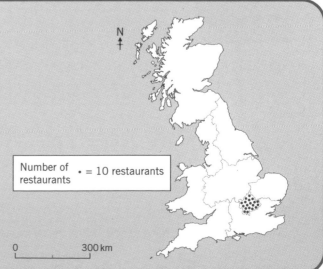

Number of restaurants   • = 10 restaurants

0   300 km

Investigating McDonald's around the world

McDonald's is a **transnational** company. This means that it does business all over the world. In 2000, McDonald's had more than 26 000 restaurants worldwide in 119 countries on six continents. This means that every minute of the day someone is eating a McDonald's for their lunch!

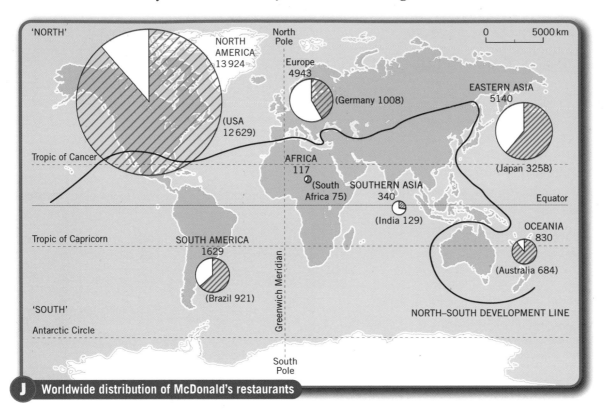

J | **Worldwide distribution of McDonald's restaurants**

Map **J** shows some of the countries where McDonald's have restaurants. It also shows the total numbers of restaurants for each continent. The world has been divided into two by the **North–South Development Line**. This is an imaginary line that separates More Economically Developed Countries (the richer countries, mainly in North America, Europe and Oceania) from the Less Economically Developed Countries. These are the poorer countries, mainly in South America, Asia and Africa.

Activities

1. Study the map. Do you notice any difference between 'North' and 'South'?

2. Use the writing frame to describe the distribution of the restaurants.

Worldwide distribution of McDonald's restaurants

McDonald's have restaurants in the continents of _____

They have very few restaurants in _____

This is because_____

On the other hand, they have many restaurants in _____

This is because _____

Step 4: Drawing conclusions

By this stage in your enquiry you have collected all the information you need to answer your question. You have displayed the results as a series of graphs, maps and diagrams, explaining what these show. You must now come to some conclusions about them.

A conclusion:

- looks at all the work you have done
- links the results to the questions you asked at the beginning
- evaluates the strengths and weaknesses of the work as a whole
- makes suggestions about further investigations you might carry out.

Our main enquiry question was:

Why are fast food restaurants located where they are?

In your conclusion you should:

> *Give the features of a fast food restaurant.*
> *Say which you think are the most important.*

> *Describe the distribution of fast food restaurants in a town centre.*

> *Summarise the results of your questionnaire, saying what people think about fast food restaurants.*

> *Describe and give reasons for the distribution of McDonald's restaurants around the world.*

help!

You may want to start your conclusion something like this:

> From our study of fast food restaurants it is clear that they have many features which make them different from other types of café or restaurant. The most important features are the things which allow the food to be served quickly and conveniently. For example, the restaurants are self-service, they have many service tills ...

Presenting your conclusions in different ways

A conclusion is not often the place where you present more graphs or maps. It is usually only writing. But sometimes it is possible to use a diagram or photograph which presents your information with more impact. The boxes show three ways of making your conclusions clearer.

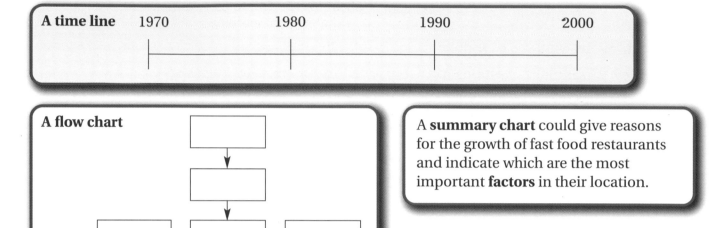

A time line 1970 1980 1990 2000

A flow chart

A **summary chart** could give reasons for the growth of fast food restaurants and indicate which are the most important **factors** in their location.

Evaluating your work

An **evaluation** of your work should finish off your enquiry.
It refers to the whole of the project and should look at the *strengths,* such as:

⊚ what you found most interesting or useful in your work

⊚ what you think went well.

It also looks at the *weaknesses*:

⊚ the problems or difficulties you had collecting information

⊚ if it would have been better to collect more or different information.

You can also suggest ideas for further investigations:

⊚ Would a study of another fast food chain like Wimpy or Harry Ramsden's give you the same results?

⊚ In what ways would the locations of Drive-thru restaurants be different?

Activities

Research activity

① What do we know, think and feel about other places?

  a Choose a place mentioned in this unit that you would like to visit.

  b Find out all you can about it. Use all the resources you have used in this unit, such as atlases, newspapers, CD-ROMS, Internet and textbooks. (ICT)

  c Prepare a brochure for tourists telling them what the place is like. Illustrate it with pictures, maps and diagrams.

Review and reflect

Activities

1 You can now use all the things you have learned about in this unit to carry out an investigation about the place where you live. Follow the route to enquiry:

1 Asking questions – How is our place connected to other places?

2 Collecting information – make up a questionnaire to ask people you know about the connections they have with other places. You could ask where their parents were born, where they go on holiday, or where they shop. *Use the work you did on page 12 to help you with this.*

3 Showing your results – use the results of your survey to make maps and diagrams to show what you have found out. Write a description of what they show. *Look back at the writing frames used to describe patterns on pages 15–16.*

4 Drawing conclusions – look back at the original question and explain what you have found out about your place's connections to other places. Remember to say what part of your enquiry went well and what part could have been improved. *Some ideas for this were given on page 18.*

Things you have learned about	Pages	Examples
Using an atlas		Finding places in north-west England
Measuring distances on maps		Finding how far to walk between restaurants in a city centre
Finding places using latitude and longitude	8–9	Giving the location of the pictures
Planning routes on maps		
Describing patterns on maps		
Drawing annotated sketches		
Carrying out an enquiry		

2 Make a large copy of the table. Fill in the things you have learned about or done for each of the parts of this unit. Examples have been given to help you.

3 Write down three important skills you have learnt from this unit and explain why you chose them.

4 Write down two things that you did or learned that might be useful later on in your geography studies, for example, measuring distances on maps.

5 Write down any activities you found difficult, and say why.

2 Restless Earth

Earthquakes and volcanoes

Learn about

A volcanic eruption or an earthquake can be disastrous, especially if it is in a place where many people live. Understanding the causes and effects of volcanoes and earthquakes can help people to manage the problems that they cause. In this unit you will learn:

- what volcanoes and earthquakes are and where they occur
- what happens when a volcano erupts
- how volcanic eruptions affect different places in the world in different ways
- what happens in an earthquake
- how people can try to reduce the effects of earthquakes
- how aid can help earthquake and volcano victims
- why people want to live in active zones.

Activities

Discussion activity

1. Look carefully at the photographs on these two pages.

   a Which do you think are about **earthquakes** and which are about **volcanoes**? What are your reasons for thinking this?

   b For each photograph, agree on at least two things it tells you about earthquakes or volcanoes.

   c Do the photographs show the *causes* or the *effects* of earthquakes and volcanoes?

2. These are all dramatic or negative images about earthquakes and volcanoes. What positive effects do you think earthquakes and volcanoes can have on people and places?

3. Start to create a word bank of the key words and terms you have used – begin with *earthquake*, *volcano*, *cause* and *effect*.

Where do volcanoes and earthquakes occur?

Activities

Research activity

1. Find out about volcanoes from around the world that have **erupted** since 1900. You could use a CD-ROM or a website on the Internet, such as http://volcano.und.nodak.edu. Use the information to create a fact file like the one below. **ICT**

Volcano location	Volcano name	Year of eruption	Latitude and longitude		Height
Philippines	Mayon	2000	13°N	123°E	2462 m
Montserrat, West Indies	Soufriere Hills	1999	16°N	62°W	915 m
Sicily, Italy	Etna	1999	37°N	15°E	3350 m
Mexico	Popocatepetl	1999	19°N	98°W	5465 m

2. Find out about earthquakes from around the world since 1900. You could use a CD-ROM or a website on the Internet, such as http://wwwneic.cr.usgs.gov. Use the information to create a fact file like the one below. **ICT**

Earthquake location	Year	Latitude and longitude		Magnitude (strength)
Taiwan	2000	26°N	124°E	6.0
Japan	2000	40°N	143°E	4.5
Iran	1999	28°N	57°E	6.5
Fiji	1998	15°S	179°W	6.7
Mexico	1995	19°N	104°W	8.0
Chile	1995	23°S	70°W	8.0
India	1950	28°N	96°E	8.6

3. Plot the volcanoes and earthquakes from your fact files onto a world map. Choose one symbol for volcanoes and a different one for earthquakes.

4. Draw a key and give the map a title that includes these words: *world, location, volcanoes, earthquakes*.

5. Write down definitions for the following words in your glossary: **location**, *erupt*, **magnitude**.

6. ### Extension

   ⊚ Invent a way of showing the height of each volcano on your map.

   ⊚ Invent a way of showing the magnitude (strength) of each earthquake on your map.

In geography it is important to be able to recognise and describe patterns on the Earth's surface. Unfortunately the world map you have drawn does not include enough volcanoes and earthquakes for any patterns to show up clearly. If you had the time to plot all the major earthquakes and volcanic eruptions that have happened over the last hundred years, some interesting patterns would be clear. Have a look at the map below, which shows more of the world's strongest earthquakes and active volcanoes.

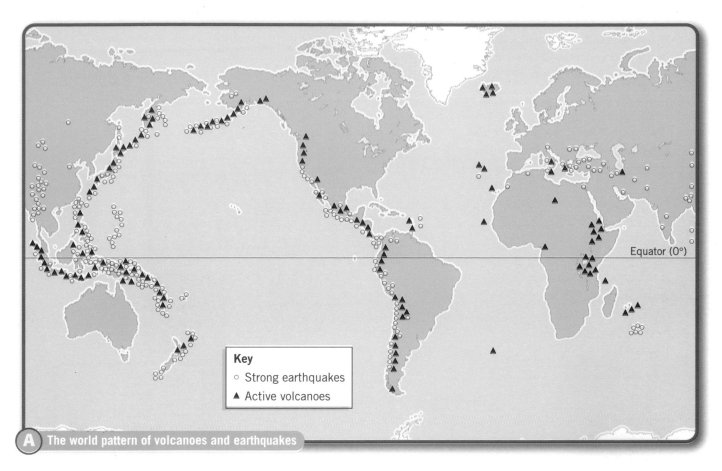

Key
○ Strong earthquakes
▲ Active volcanoes

Equator (0°)

A The world pattern of volcanoes and earthquakes

Activities 📖

① Write a definition for the word *describe*.

② Create a word list which would help to describe the volcano and earthquake distribution patterns shown on map **A**.

③ Write a description of the world distribution of volcanoes and earthquakes using the words from your word list. Use the *How to ...* box to help you to write a good geographical description.

How to ...

... describe patterns on maps

◎ Begin with a **general statement**, e.g. *'The map shows that volcanoes and earthquakes are found ...'*.

◎ Go on to give greater **detail** about where in the world they are and are not found.

◎ Include **place names**, e.g. *countries, continents, seas, oceans, mountain ranges ...*

◎ Mention **directions** for the patterns: *... north to south, ... to the south-west*, etc.

Why do volcanoes and earthquakes occur where they do?

The Earth has a thin **crust**. Scientists think that this crust is divided up into a number of different-sized sections, called **tectonic plates**, which move slowly in different directions. Some, like the North American and Eurasian Plates, are moving away from one another. Others, like the Nazca and South American Plates, are moving towards each other. Finally, in some parts of the world the plates are moving sideways past each other, as along the San Andreas Fault in the western USA. Earthquakes and volcanoes occur mainly in **active zones** at the edges of tectonic plates.

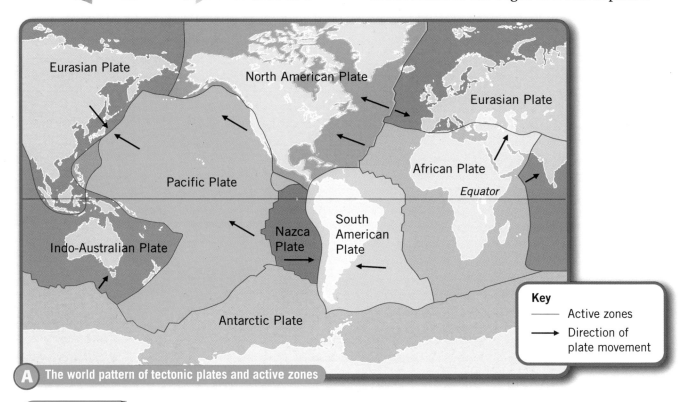

A The world pattern of tectonic plates and active zones

Key
— Active zones
→ Direction of plate movement

Activities

1. Table **B** compares the world pattern of volcanoes and earthquakes with the world pattern of tectonic plates and active zones. Look back at map **A** on page 23 to find an example of the pattern of volcanoes and earthquakes. Now look at map **A** on this page to find an example that matches. Add these to the ones already done for you on a copy of the table.

B

World pattern of volcanoes and earthquakes	World pattern of tectonic plates and active zones
Earthquakes and volcanoes occur in **linear** patterns in some parts of the world.	Active zones are found around the edges of the world's tectonic plates.
A belt of volcanoes and earthquakes is located along the west coast of South America.	There is an active zone where the Nazca and South American Plates move together.
Volcanoes and earthquakes occur along the west coast of North America.	In places, the North American and the Pacific Plates move past one another.

2. Look again at the maps and your table. What have you found out about the links between the world patterns of volcanoes and earthquakes and the world pattern of tectonic plates?

What are volcanoes?

Volcanoes are openings (**vents**) in the Earth's crust where **magma** (molten rock) from inside the Earth is able to escape to the surface. The magma can appear in a number of different forms:

- as liquid **lava** (molten rock) that flows down the volcano sides

- as **volcanic bombs** – lumps of molten rock that solidify as they fall from the sky

- as hot ash and dust which are thrown into the air and eventually settle on the surrounding land

- as steam and gases, which may be poisonous.

Volcanic eruptions are strongly influenced by the type of magma that escapes. Some are very explosive and dangerous. When Mount Pinatubo in the Philippines erupted in 1991, it sent up a cloud of ash and steam 30 km high. About 700 people died as a result of the eruption.

Other eruptions are more gentle. Kilauea, one of the Hawaiian Islands, has been continuously pouring out runny lava since 1983 with little threat to humans.

Volcanoes may be active, dormant or extinct.

- **Active volcanoes** are those that have erupted within historical time and are likely to erupt again. There are over 700 active volcanoes in the world.

- **Dormant volcanoes** are currently inactive but may erupt again. Most of the Cascade volcanoes on the west coast of North America are believed to be dormant.

- **Extinct volcanoes** are those that are unlikely to erupt again in the future. There are a number of extinct volcanoes in Britain, such as the one Edinburgh Castle is built on.

A Volcanic eruption on the island of Heimaey, Iceland

Activities

1. Use photograph **A** to draw a 'wordscape'.

   First draw a simple outline sketch. Include outlines of the main features.

2. Next, choose nouns and adjectives that describe the different areas of the photograph.

3. Carefully write the words onto the outline sketch. Shape the words to fit the features in the photograph they describe.

What happens when a volcano erupts?

The Philippine Islands are located in an active zone on the edges of the Eurasian and Philippine Plates. This active zone is part of the 'Pacific Ring of Fire' where there are many volcanoes and earthquakes. Mount Pinatubo is one of 22 active volcanoes in the Philippines and is located about 100 km north-west of the capital city, Manila. After being dormant for more than 600 years, Pinatubo awoke with a bang on 9 June 1991. It caused one of the largest eruptions of the twentieth century.

A The location of Mount Pinatubo

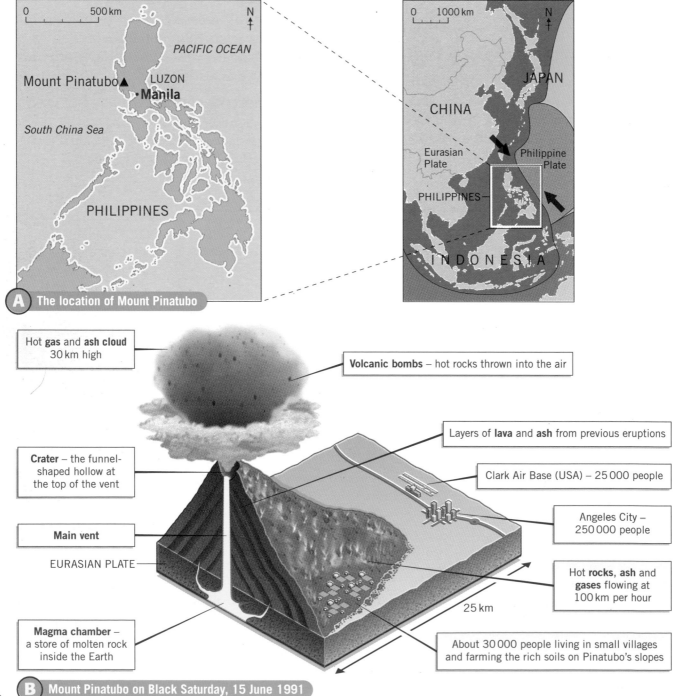

- Hot **gas** and **ash cloud** 30 km high
- **Volcanic bombs** – hot rocks thrown into the air
- **Crater** – the funnel-shaped hollow at the top of the vent
- Layers of **lava** and **ash** from previous eruptions
- Clark Air Base (USA) – 25 000 people
- **Main vent**
- EURASIAN PLATE
- Angeles City – 250 000 people
- Hot **rocks, ash** and **gases** flowing at 100 km per hour
- 25 km
- **Magma chamber** – a store of molten rock inside the Earth
- About 30 000 people living in small villages and farming the rich soils on Pinatubo's slopes

B Mount Pinatubo on Black Saturday, 15 June 1991

26

Case Study

The eruption of Mount Pinatubo

Extracts from the diary of Kimi Nath

C The eruption of Mount Pinatubo

When the Angeles City newspapers reported that a group of American volcano scientists had moved into the Clark Air Base, everyone was talking about Mount Pinatubo and saying, 'What volcano?' Many Filipinos had never heard of the volcano, which had been dormant for over 600 years.

Wednesday 12 June
Mount Pinatubo gave us the first taste of her fury. A deep, rumbling boom shook the earth, and an angry, dark cloud appeared in the distance. A cold wind blew around us. It was very eerie.

As the 'cloud' moved towards us, it spread out and the sun disappeared. Dust began to fall from the sky. By the time the 'cloud' drifted past us, 2 cm of ash coated the ground. The same thing happened on Thursday, and on Friday. Everyone was tense, wondering what would happen next. We didn't have to wait long before we found out.

D Ash on the cars at Clark Air Base

Saturday 15 June
The sun was shining brightly at 8.30 a.m. After clearing 5 to 6 cm of ash from my car, I drove to the Clark Air Base, just north of Angeles City, for a meeting. Around 9.00 a.m. a huge rumble shook the room, and the sky began to darken. By 9.30 it was midnight black. By a cruel twist of fate, a huge typhoon hit at the same time. Swirling winds mixed the heavy rain with ash so that mud fell from the sky. The force of the eruption was so strong that huge pieces of the volcano blew apart, so that rocks also rained down. Electricity, water and telephones all failed, so we sat in darkness. The muddy ash came down more heavily with each passing moment, and the 'rotten eggs' stench from the sulphur in the air made us sick. Sulphur fireballs shot blazing orange through the night, and the typhoon brought lightning, which exploded in fiery displays. Then the earthquakes began ... They came one after another, shifting the ground beneath us. Some were powerful enough to send things crashing to the ground and to crack the beams of the homes in which we huddled. With the awful storm outside and the earthquakes within, there was no safe place to go. Throughout 'Black Saturday' we huddled in fear and wondered if the world was truly coming to an end.

Sunday 16 June
We came out of our shelters cautiously and looked in awe on the grey devastation all around us. Our homes were buried in ash and hundreds of buildings had collapsed. Roads were blocked by mud, trees and vehicles; the power was still off and there wasn't much food or water. We knew things were never going to get back to normal ...

E Clark Air Base during the eruption

Pinatubo leaves behind a wasteland

Pinatubo's ash, dust and **lahars** (mudflows) have turned vast areas of farmland into a wasteland. The eruption has affected more than 249 000 families (1.2 million people), causing over 700 deaths and 184 injuries. Many more might have died, but fortunately warnings based on information from **seismographs** at the American Clark Air Base allowed the authorities to evacuate about 14 000 people from the area surrounding the volcano.

Water supplies, power lines, roads and bridges were badly damaged by the lahars. Houses and public buildings collapsed from the weight of ash. More than 650 000 workers are out of work because of the destruction of their farms, shops and factories.

The Americans were forced to evacuate Clark Air Base after volcanic dust, ash and lahars left its runways useless and endangered its planes. In Manila, 100 km away, the International Airport was also closed for four days and public buildings were turned into evacuation centres to house refugees from the devastated areas.

F Extract from *The Philippine Star*, 21 July 1991

G Mount Pinatubo's new crater lake, formed after the 1991 eruption

H Whole villages were covered in ash

Lahars swept away whole villages. Green rice paddies and sugar-cane fields were covered with ash. About 4000 square kilometres were affected, but people have since returned to farm the rich soils formed from the mud and ash.

I

Pinatubo's eruption threw 20 million tonnes of sulphur dioxide into the air. Scientists think that this caused a 1°C fall in global temperatures for over five years. The dust thrown into the atmosphere by Pinatubo may also add to global warming in the future.

J

Wildlife returns to Mount Pinatubo

Eight years after Pinatubo's hot gases stripped its trees of life and ash blanketed its slopes, wild cats, boars, deer and monkeys are returning to areas where plants have started to grow again. Snakes, such as boa constrictors and cobras, and even monitor lizards are also appearing on the volcano's slopes.

K Extract from article by Ding Cervantes, 20 April 1999

This **satellite image** of the area around Mount Pinatubo was taken by the space shuttle Endeavour on 13 April 1994. The main **crater** and its lake can easily be seen in *blue*. The *pale pink* colour on the slopes of Pinatubo shows the ash deposited during the 1991 eruption. The *dark pink* areas show the lahars. These are still a hazard to the people who have returned to farm the area around the volcano. Every time rain falls on Mount Pinatubo, mud slides down from the highlands *(dark green)* on to villages, homes and fields. On the western side of the image the lahars spill into the South China Sea *(black)*. Satellite images can be very helpful in monitoring hazards such as lahars. This can stop lives being lost.

L A 'false-colour' satellite image of the area around Pinatubo

Angeles City
– well on the road to recovery

In 1990 Angeles City, 25 km to the east of Pinatubo, had a population of 250 000. Many of its industries supported the American Clark Air Base, just outside the city. When the 25 000 people living at the Air Base left after the eruption, farmers, furniture-makers, tailors, restaurants, auto-repair shops, hotels and night clubs, taxi-drivers, etc. were left without customers. Over 250 000 people lost their jobs as a result of the eruption of Pinatubo.

M Angeles City

After 1991, Angeles City began to grow as a tourist destination. It now has 24 restaurants, six new hotels, 30 night clubs, four Internet cafés and hundreds of small boutiques, pharmacies, photo shops and taxi companies, employing thousands of Filipinos. The tourist industry is now the biggest employer in the area. The government is spending large sums of money on attracting foreign visitors.

Activity

1 You have been asked by the Angeles City Tourist Information Office to produce a brochure for visitors to the region to inform them about the eruption of Mount Pinatubo in 1991. The brochure must include:

- ◎ an annotated cross-section showing what happened when Mount Pinatubo erupted

- ◎ an annotated map of the Pinatubo region locating features of the eruption

- ◎ written information about the area before, during and after the eruption

- ◎ a glossary of terms to help tourists understand exactly what happened and why

- ◎ illustrations that capture tourists' interest in the volcano – guides in Angeles City earn 300 Pesos (about £5) for each tour party they take up Mount Pinatubo.

help!

When you write your brochure, remember that good geographers:

- ✪ include specific facts, figures and place names in their work
- ✪ write information in their own words
- ✪ evaluate their work when it is finished.

What happens in an earthquake?

The Earth is made up of three main layers – the crust, the **mantle** and the **core**. The crust is much thinner than the other layers and is the only layer of the Earth that humans have actually seen. The crust is broken up into tectonic plates which 'float' on the mantle. They are pushed slowly in different directions by the molten rock beneath. Active zones are created where tectonic plates move past one another. Earthquakes and volcanoes tend to occur in these zones.

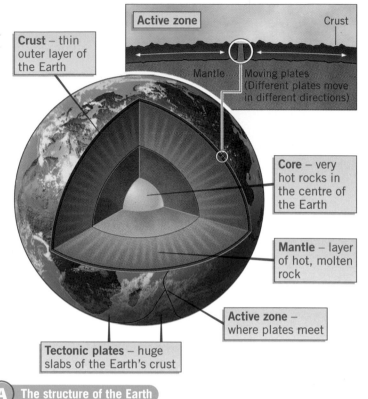

Active zone
Crust

Crust – thin outer layer of the Earth

Mantle   Moving plates (Different plates move in different directions)

Core – very hot rocks in the centre of the Earth

Mantle – layer of hot, molten rock

Active zone – where plates meet

Tectonic plates – huge slabs of the Earth's crust

A The structure of the Earth

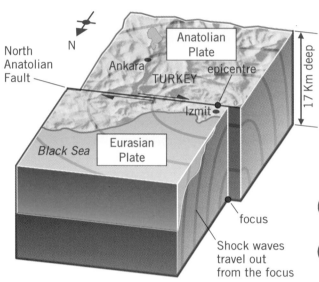

North Anatolian Fault

N

Anatolian Plate

Ankara

epicentre

TURKEY

Izmit

17 Km deep

Black Sea

Eurasian Plate

focus

Shock waves travel out from the focus

B The Izmit earthquake in Turkey, 17 August 1999

Earthquakes are caused when two plates moving past one another become 'stuck' for a while so that tension builds up. Eventually the stress becomes so great that the crust breaks and moves suddenly. The point where the rock actually breaks is called the **focus**. This is usually found far beneath the surface of the Earth. The point on the surface directly above the focus is called the **epicentre**. When the plates move suddenly, **shock waves** are sent out in all directions. These waves can cause a lot of damage on the Earth's surface.

The magnitude or strength of an earthquake is measured using an instrument called a seismograph which records the shaking of the ground. Look at the seismogram **C** for the Turkish earthquake in 1999. The magnitude is shown by the lines that go up and down. The stronger the quake, the

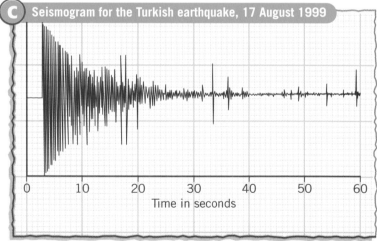

C Seismogram for the Turkish earthquake, 17 August 1999

0   10   20   30   40   50   60
Time in seconds

longer will be the lines drawn on the graph. The length of time that a quake lasts is shown by the horizontal distance across the graph.

The magnitude of an earthquake can be measured using the **Richter Scale** (see **D**). Each point on the scale is actually ten times bigger than the one below it. This means that an earthquake measuring 6 on the Richter scale is ten times stronger than one measuring 5. Earthquakes below 2.5 are not usually felt by humans.

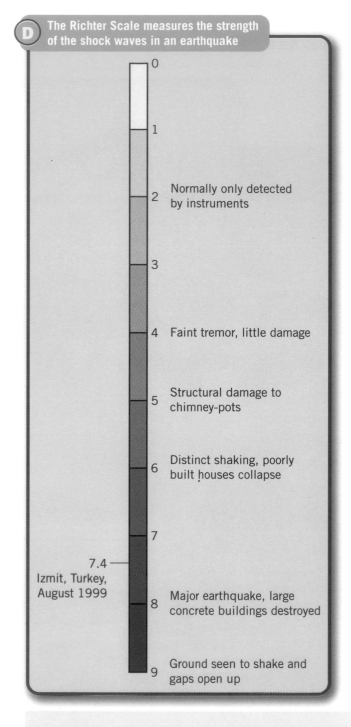

D The Richter Scale measures the strength of the shock waves in an earthquake

0

1

2 — Normally only detected by instruments

3

4 — Faint tremor, little damage

5 — Structural damage to chimney-pots

6 — Distinct shaking, poorly built houses collapse

7

7.4 — Izmit, Turkey, August 1999

8 — Major earthquake, large concrete buildings destroyed

9 — Ground seen to shake and gaps open up

Activities

① Copy out the passage below. Fill in the missing words to explain why the Izmit earthquake in Turkey in 1999 happened.

A huge earthquake measuring _____ on the Richter Scale happened in Turkey on 17 August 1999. It was caused when two plates, the _____ Plate and the _____ Plate, became 'stuck' for a while. This caused stress to build up until the Earth's crust eventually broke, sending out _____ in all directions. The focus of the earthquake was about _____ below the Earth's surface. The earthquake lasted for about _____ seconds and was most violent during the first _____ seconds. Earthquakes and volcanoes often happen in active zones such as the _____ Fault.

Research activities

② Find the name of a scale, other than the Richter Scale, which is used to measure earthquakes.

③ Download a map from the Internet showing the most recent earthquakes in the world. Use one of the following sites: **ICT**

http://www.geo.arizona.edu

http://wwwneic.cr.usgs.gov

a Draw a table like the one below. Fill in the details for each earthquake.

Country	Date	Magnitude	Depth

b Give the table a suitable title.

c How many of the earthquakes in your table have reached the national news?

d Why do you think this is the case?

How do earthquakes affect people and places?

Activities

Look at the photographs on this page and on pages 20 and 21. They suggest some of the ways in which earthquakes affect people's lives and the places they live. Use them to help you answer these questions. Try to add your own ideas as well.

1. Write down five sentences that describe how earthquakes affect people's lives and how people feel after an earthquake.

2. Now write down five sentences that describe how earthquakes affect places – buildings, transport links, services such as hospitals, electricity supplies, etc.

3. Compare your lists with those of another person. Add at least three of their ideas to your own.

4. Next, rank your list for question **1** according to how severely an earthquake would affect *your* family. Write down the effect that would have the most impact first.

5. Now rank your list for question **2** in the same way.

6. Look at the top two effects in each list. Explain why you decided that these would have the greatest impact.

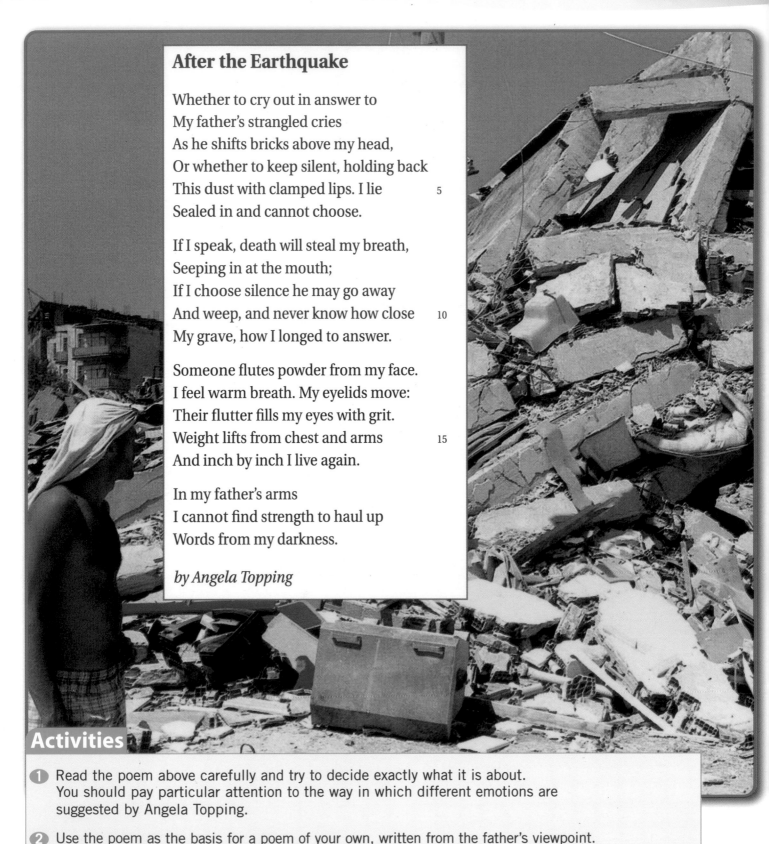

After the Earthquake

Whether to cry out in answer to
My father's strangled cries
As he shifts bricks above my head,
Or whether to keep silent, holding back
This dust with clamped lips. I lie   5
Sealed in and cannot choose.

If I speak, death will steal my breath,
Seeping in at the mouth;
If I choose silence he may go away
And weep, and never know how close   10
My grave, how I longed to answer.

Someone flutes powder from my face.
I feel warm breath. My eyelids move:
Their flutter fills my eyes with grit.
Weight lifts from chest and arms   15
And inch by inch I live again.

In my father's arms
I cannot find strength to haul up
Words from my darkness.

by Angela Topping

Activities

① Read the poem above carefully and try to decide exactly what it is about.
You should pay particular attention to the way in which different emotions are
suggested by Angela Topping.

② Use the poem as the basis for a poem of your own, written from the father's viewpoint.
It should suggest the emotions he feels as he searches for, and eventually finds,
his buried child.

  a Begin by creating a list of words which could be used to describe the father's changing
  feelings as he digs through the rubble.

  b Try to use the structure of the poem above to suggest that what the father feels mirrors
  the feelings of his child.

Case Study

What happened in the 1999 earthquake in Turkey?

A The location of the earthquake

On Tuesday 17 August 1999 at 3 a.m. a strong earthquake hit north-west Turkey. Its epicentre was close to the city of Izmit, 55 km south-east of Istanbul (see map A).

The information on pages 35–38 comes from a variety of sources written at different times over the months following the earthquake.

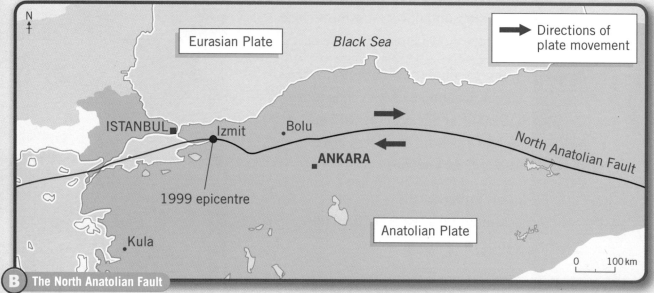

B The North Anatolian Fault

The earthquake's epicentre was about 11 km south-east of the city of Izmit. It was caused by the movement of the Eurasian Plate (moving east) and the Anatolian Plate (moving west) in an active zone known as the North Anatolian Fault (see map **B**). In places the plates moved up to 5 metres in opposite directions. The effects of this could be seen on roads and railways that crossed the North Anatolian Fault (see photo **D**).

The earthquake measured 7.4 on the Richter Scale. It happened 17 km below the Earth's surface. Shallow earthquakes are often more powerful than deeper ones because there is less of the Earth's crust above them to absorb the force.

C *Report from The National Earthquake Information Centre*

D A railway crossing the North Anatolian Fault

Terror in Turkey: quake kills more than 2000

The worst recorded earthquake to hit Turkey killed at least 2000 people and injured thousands today. It destroyed buildings and cut off power and water to millions living in the area.

The quake struck at 3 o'clock this morning, while most people were still asleep. The lucky ones ran into the street in panic; others were crushed in the rubble. Many fled their homes in nightclothes and without shoes. Later, they walked through the glass-strewn streets with cloth wrapped around their feet.

Dozens of buildings and highway overpasses collapsed in Istanbul, and many roads were severely damaged and unusable.

With the city's rescue services stretched to the limit, it was mostly neighbours and relatives who fought to pull people from the wreckage.

Local people working under car headlights in the early hours used their bare hands to try to dig people out of the rubble, while the young and elderly slept in the open.

The USA, France, Germany, Switzerland, Italy, Japan and Israel have all offered help, but rescue teams with special equipment and sniffer dogs will take time to get to Turkey.

Hospitals in Izmit have been turning away people with minor injuries and treating people on pavements. Medical workers have been breaking chemists' windows to get supplies.

E Newspaper report, 17 August 1999

Dead	Injured	People homeless	People living on the streets
15 135	23 983	600 000	200 000

F Casualty assessment report by Government Crisis Centre, 6 September 1999

Place	Date	Magnitude	Deaths
Turkey	1999	7.4	15 135
Afghanistan	1998	7.1	5000
Afghanistan	1998	6.4	4000
Iran	1997	7.1	1613
Russia	1995	7.5	1841
Japan	1995	7.2	6424
India	1993	6.4	7801
Indonesia	1992	6.8	2000
India	1991	6.1	1500
Afghanistan	1991	6.8	1500
Philippines	1990	7.7	1641
Iran	1990	7.7	40 000

G The worst earthquakes of the 1990s

I heard a deep thump and a few seconds later the whole house started shaking like crazy. We had a hard time running down the stairs, getting tossed from one side to the other. It did not stop for 45 seconds. When we reached the garden I saw the water in the swimming pool getting splashed around as if a ship was going through it. Tiles around the pool were shooting 1-2 metres up into the air. Then it stopped.

Minutes after the quake the entire city was without power. I saw a starry sky for the first time in more than a decade as the city was in total darkness, apart from the headlights of the cars driving around aimlessly ...

This is the first time I have ever felt so close to dying. You feel so helpless ... nothing you can do. Now I know that nothing is permanent in the world.

Kadir Bahcecik, Istanbul

H E-mail sent to a website for those wishing to contact family and friends after the earthquake

'I have been crying for two nights and no one has come to save my family,' shouted Mehmet, as he burst into the mayor's office with tears streaming down his face. 'If you don't come to my house soon, I will dynamite it myself to free them!' Anger, desperation and grief had carved deep lines around his mouth. He, like thousands of others, can't understand why there isn't a crane on every heap of rubble searching for those still missing.

I   Television news report, 20 August 1999

SHODDILY BUILT HOUSES COLLAPSE IN QUAKE

There has been growing public anger that so many buildings fell down because precautions against earthquakes had not been taken.

In recent years, officials have turned a blind eye to builders who have skimped on materials to provide housing for the flood of people moving in from the countryside.

In the town of Duzce, 33 people thought to be responsible for the collapse of several buildings have been arrested. One of them admitted to mixing salty sea water with concrete. This caused buildings to crumble when the quake hit.

Buildings constructed over the past five years, using Turkey's earthquake building code, seem to have survived the quake much better.

J   Newspaper report, 23 August 1999

40 000 FEARED DEAD IN TURKISH QUAKE

Fears are growing that the death toll from Turkey's devastating earthquake could eventually reach 40 000, making it the country's worst this century.

More than 10 000 people are already known to have died and another 45 000 people have been injured. The Turkish authorities are predicting that thousands more bodies will be found beneath the rubble.

Rescuers breaking iron bars to reach a trapped woman

Concern is growing for the health of those who have lived through the quake, with disease the latest threat to survivors. The fear of aftershocks has persuaded millions of people to camp out in the open – close to the rotting bodies of those killed in the earthquake. 'The greatest problem now facing us is that of disease,' Prime Minister Ecevit told reporters.

Most rescue workers are wearing masks, and are being immunised against typhoid. Cholera cases are being reported in some areas.

K   Newspaper report, 20 August 1999

Houses damaged beyond repair
120 000
Houses heavily damaged
50 000
Other collapsed buildings
2000
Other heavily damaged buildings
4000

L   Building damage assessment, as reported by Government Crisis Centre, 6 September 1999

The earthquake damaged buildings from Istanbul to Bolu (a distance of 250 km). Nearly 70 per cent of the buildings in the cities of Golcuk, Izmit, Topcular and Kular fell down. Most deaths and injuries were caused by collapsing buildings.

While most buildings were damaged by the shaking of the ground, on the coast waves rushed in as the ground sank and washed houses into the sea. Many of the collapsed buildings were four to eight storeys high and built of reinforced concrete.

Buildings collapsed as a result of:

- poor concrete quality
- poor reinforcement
- building alterations (e.g. an added floor)
- badly prepared building sites.

It will cost about £3.4 billion to rebuild the destroyed buildings.

M Report by the Earthquake Engineering Research Institute

Winter thoughts weigh heavily on the homeless

Ankle-deep in mud, in tent cities swamped by rain, homeless quake survivors wonder whether they will have a sturdy roof over their heads by winter, now just two months away. Unfortunately, the odds are against them – 600 000 people have been left homeless. Although the government has announced the building of 200 000 new homes, these will take up to three years to complete. People whose houses are declared safe have been asked to return home.

N Newspaper report, 27 August 1999

O Newspaper report, September 1999

NEW SYSTEMS CONSIDERED

Mindful of dangers from new quakes, Turkey has been considering new preparation measures. The *Milliyet* newspaper reported today that the government would spend £2 million on an early-warning system for Istanbul, a city of 12 million people.

It said the system would provide an early warning of shock waves, allow damaged buildings to be checked quickly, and help to prevent gas leaks that could cause fires.

Activities

1. Write a script for a five-minute television news report on '*Why did so many people die in the Turkish earthquake?*'. It is to be broadcast one month after the earthquake. Include sections of information about:
   - the *cause* of the earthquake
   - the *effects* of the earthquake (on the people and the places)
   - the *responses* of the government and emergency services to the earthquake
   - how the Turkish government plans to *prevent* so many deaths next time.

2. Begin each section of the report with an enquiry question. For example, the first section might start with:

   What was the cause of the Turkish earthquake of 1999?

3. Your report should also contain:
   - location maps at different scales, labelled with information about the earthquake
   - eye-catching graphs and diagrams showing relevant data
   - memorable images (such as photographs)
   - stories about 'real' people affected by the earthquake – these help to capture the imagination of the viewers.

help!

Good geographers:

- think carefully about the best ways of presenting information
- write information in their own words
- alter the way information is presented, e.g. change tables into graphs or maps
- annotate or label maps, photographs and diagrams
- carry out their own research into enquiry questions.

How can people make earthquakes less of a hazard?

Scientists still cannot say when or where an earthquake will strike. Successful earthquake **prediction** is very rare. A famous example was the Haicheng earthquake in China in 1976. Local people reported early-warning signs, so many people were persuaded to camp outside. When a quake measuring 7.3 on the Richter Scale struck, very few people were killed. This success came from guessing correctly that an earthquake was likely to happen, and from local people taking the warnings seriously. In other parts of the world, even careful **monitoring** using seismographs has not helped. In San Francisco, USA, in 1989 and Kobe, Japan, in 1995, the quakes came without any real warning signs; in Kobe, thousands of people were killed.

In many parts of the world it is now possible to say how likely an earthquake might be. This means that people can plan to reduce the effects of earthquakes when they happen. Since 1900 nearly 3 million people have lost their lives in earthquakes. Most deaths are caused by falling bridges and buildings.

Case Study: USA

The Transamerica Pyramid in San Francisco was built to withstand earthquakes. When a magnitude 7.1 earthquake struck California in 1989 the top floors swayed more than 30 cm from side to side but the building was not damaged. No one was seriously injured.

A

Case Study: India

In rich *and* poor parts of the world, buildings are tested for their ability to survive earthquakes. In India, different types of houses were built on a concrete platform on wheels. This was shaken by a tractor to show which house would survive an earthquake best.

B

Case Study: Peru

The government has trained local people to build cheap and simple earthquake-proof buildings. The design shown in **C** is a rectangular house built of bamboo covered with mud. The roof is made of timber and thatch. The people are very poor, so it was important to use local materials with a long life. The bamboo and wooden frame is flexible, making it earthquake-resistant. The mud-covered walls rest on a low foundation to protect them from ground water.

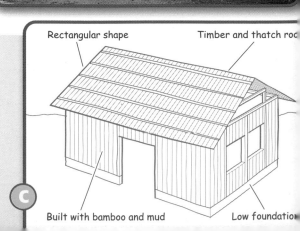

Rectangular shape   Timber and thatch roo

C

Built with bamboo and mud   Low foundation

Case Study: West Coast, USA
Preparing an earthquake plan

- Choose a safe place in every room – under a table or against an inside wall where nothing can fall on you.

- Practise DROP, COVER, AND HOLD ON at least twice a year. Drop under a table, hold on, and protect your eyes.

- Find out ways you can protect your home, such as bolting the house to its foundation.

- Take a first-aid class.

- Train in how to use a fire extinguisher.

- Bolt bookcases, china cabinets and other tall furniture to the wall. Put strong latches on cupboards. Strap the water heater to the wall.

- Prepare a Disaster Kit for the home and car containing:

  – first-aid kit

  – canned food and can-opener

  – fifteen litres of water per person

  – protective clothing and sleeping-bags

  – radio, flashlight and batteries

  – written instructions for how to turn off gas, electricity and water.

D

Rich *and* poor countries carry out earthquake drills. These Californian schoolchildren are practising an earthquake drill.

F

Monitoring how structures behave

Scientists have put instruments into dams, bridges, pipelines, roads and buildings to monitor how they behave during earthquakes. The man in the photo below is checking earthquake monitoring equipment in California.

E

Activities

1. Locate the countries in the case studies on these two pages on an outline world map. Add an annotation box about each case study.

2. In each box describe what is being done and explain how this can help to reduce the effects of earthquakes.

3. The different ways of reducing the effects of earthquakes can be classified according to whether they involve:

   - educating people about what to do before, during or after an earthquake
   - improving buildings through better design and construction
   - monitoring earth movements.

   Shade the annotation boxes in three different colours according to which classification they match. Some boxes may require more than one colour.

4. Add a key and a title to your map.

5. **Extension**
   Find out about other case studies for different parts of the world.
   a Annotate the case studies onto your world map.
   b Colour the annotation boxes to classify each way of reducing earthquake effects.

How can aid help the victims of earthquakes and volcanoes?

One way of helping countries that have been affected by earthquakes or volcanic eruptions is to give them **aid**. Aid can be given in many different forms. Some of these are shown in **A**.

The **donor**, which gives the aid, is usually a rich country. The **recipient**, which receives the aid, is often a poorer country. Aid is one way for wealthy countries to help poorer countries.

There are two main types of aid:

◉ **Official aid:** this is given by a government and paid for by the taxpayers of the donor country.

◉ **Voluntary aid:** this is provided by charities such as Oxfam, the Red Cross and Christian Aid.

Aid can be given in two ways:

◉ **Short-term emergency relief aid:** this is used to help solve immediate problems such as those caused by earthquakes, volcanic eruptions, floods or wars. It is sometimes called humanitarian aid.

◉ **Long-term development aid:** this gives people access to basic needs such as clean water and reliable food production. Long-term aid should help to improve living standards so that a country can develop.

Money to pay for supplies or rebuilding programmes, e.g. housing, roads, energy

Technology, e.g. heat-seeking equipment or computers to help manage the relief operations

Different forms of aid

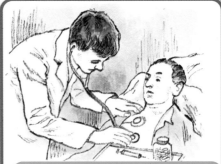
Skilled people, e.g. rescue workers, doctors and engineers, who can give advice and help people

Relief supplies: food, clothing, clean water, tents, planes and medical equipment

A

Activities (ICT)

① Look up each charity in the list below on the Internet. For each one:

a Write down its full name.

b Name the recipient countries where the charity is providing aid at the moment.

c Say whether it provides short-term aid. If so, list the types of disasters involved.

www.care.org.uk   www.cafod.org.uk   www.christian-aid.org.uk

www.unicef.org.uk   www.netaid.org   www.oxfam.org.uk

www.redcross.org.uk   www.doctorswithoutborders.org

② How do the charities differ in the forms of aid they provide?

B An American relief team's equipment arrives in Turkey

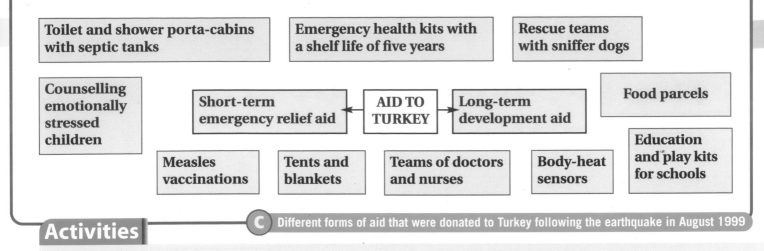

Toilet and shower porta-cabins with septic tanks	Emergency health kits with a shelf life of five years	Rescue teams with sniffer dogs
Counselling emotionally stressed children	Short-term emergency relief aid ← AID TO TURKEY → Long-term development aid	Food parcels
		Education and play kits for schools
Measles vaccinations	Tents and blankets	Teams of doctors and nurses	Body-heat sensors

C Different forms of aid that were donated to Turkey following the earthquake in August 1999

Activities

3 Make a copy of **C**. Draw an arrow from each example of aid in the pink boxes to either the short-term or the long-term aid box. If you think the example may be both short-term and long-term, draw an arrow to both blue boxes.

4 Compare your answers with one other person. Where you disagree, discuss the reasons for this.

Case Study

How has UNICEF provided aid for victims of the 1999 Turkish earthquakes?

UNICEF (United Nations Children's Fund) is a charity that supports children and helps to meet their basic needs. It aims to provide children with health care and food, clean water and education.

Seven months after the Izmit earthquake of August 1999 over 77 000 children under 8 were still homeless. Table **D** shows who donated money to UNICEF's long-term 'Recovery Plan for Turkish Children'. Table **E** shows you how the money was spent.

Where does UNICEF get its money from?

In 1998, 62 per cent of UNICEF's money came from the governments of different countries. The remaining 38 per cent came from fund-raising and the sale of greetings cards.

Groups that donated money	Amount donated (millions of US dollars)
Governments	7
UNICEF Committees	7.5
Total	14.5

D Money donated to UNICEF for the Turkish Recovery Plan

What money was spent on	Amount spent (millions of US dollars)
Water and sanitation	5
Education	4
Health	3
Emotional counselling	2.3
Transport	0.1
Children's play areas	0.1
Total	14.5

E How UNICEF spent aid money for the Recovery Plan

Activities

5 Draw two different types of graph to show the information on tables **D** and **E**. **123**

6 In what ways do your graphs show the information more clearly than the tables?

7 Which graph do you think shows the information best? Give reasons for your answer.

8 Why do you think UNICEF made water and sanitation its first priority?

9 Why might other charities have spent the money differently?

Adapted from: *UNICEF Recovery Plan for Turkish Children,* 13 March 2000

41

Why do people choose to live in active zones?

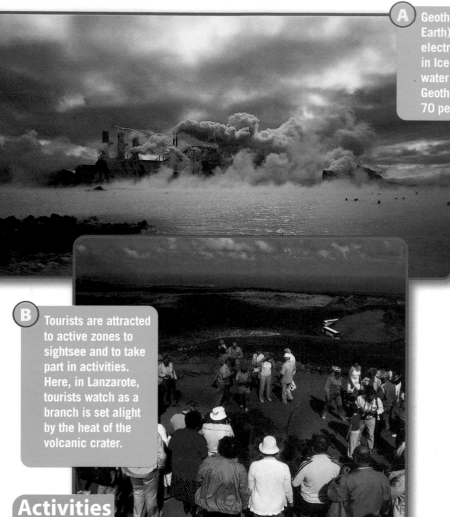

A Geothermal energy (heat from the Earth) can be used to generate electrical power. This power station in Iceland also supplies the hot spring water for the local spa resort. Geothermal heat warms more than 70 per cent of homes in Iceland.

C This grid of fields is near Mount Aso in Japan. Over thousands of years, volcanic rocks have broken down to form some of the most fertile soils on Earth.

B Tourists are attracted to active zones to sightsee and to take part in activities. Here, in Lanzarote, tourists watch as a branch is set alight by the heat of the volcanic crater.

Activities

① Draw a table like the one below.

Disadvantages of living in an active zone	Advantages of living in an active zone

② Look through this chapter and complete the left-hand column of your table with the problems of living in active zones.

③ Read the information on this page and complete the right-hand column with the good points about living in active zones.

④ Look at the two lists you have written.

  a Are there more advantages or more disadvantages?

  b Do you think the disadvantages are more important than the advantages? If so, then why?

  c Suggest problems in using only the information in this textbook to answer questions **2**, **3** and **4**.

⑤ Many people choose to live in an active zone even though it can be extremely hazardous. Why do you think this is the case?

D My family has lived on the slopes of Mount Etna for many generations. We are prepared to live with the danger because we love it here ... it is our home.

Review and reflect

Key enquiry questions	Page numbers	Case Studies	What I learned about or did
What do you already know about earthquakes and volcanoes?	20, 21		Cause and effect
Where do volcanoes and earthquakes occur?	22, 23		Located features on a map
Why do volcanoes and earthquakes occur where they do?	24		Compared patterns on two maps
What are volcanoes?	25		Created a wordscape
What happens when a volcano erupts?	26, 27, 28, 29	Mount Pinatubo, Philippines	Annotated a map and cross-section
What happens in an earthquake?	30, 31		Researched using the Internet
How do earthquakes affect people and places?	32, 33		Explained how earthquakes affect people's lives
How do people feel after an earthquake?	33		Wrote a poem on the feelings of an earthquake victim
What happened in the 1999 earthquake in Turkey?	34, 35, 36, 37	Izmit, Turkey	Researched an enquiry question
How can people make earthquakes less of a hazard?	38, 39		Described and explained
How can aid help the victims of earthquakes and volcanoes?	40, 41		Classified information
Why do people choose to live in active zones?	42		Identified problems from writing and photographs

Activities

1 Make a large copy of the table above. For each enquiry question, look back at your work for this unit and write down the names of the places you have studied in the 'Case Studies' column. Some have already been done to help you.

2 The fourth column gives at least one thing you should have learned about or done for each enquiry question. For each one, find where in your work you actually did this. Then add at least one more thing you learned. Some extra examples have been provided in the help box.

3 Write down the three most important things you have learned from your work on the Restless Earth. Explain why you chose them.

4 Write down three things you did or learned that might be useful in other subject areas. For example, writing a report would be useful in a history lesson.

5 Write down which activities you found most difficult. Give reasons for your choices.

help!

These ideas may help you to answer question **2**.

- Classification
- Research
- Writing in report genre
- Writing in recount genre
- Asking geographical questions
- Using an atlas
- Drawing graphs
- Working with others.

3 People everywhere

Learn about

The rapid increase in the population of Planet Earth is an issue that your generation will have to face. It has great consequences for large numbers of people around the world now. In this unit you will learn about:

⊚ what has happened to the world's population over the past 200 years

⊚ why the population is increasing so rapidly

⊚ what geographers mean by population density

⊚ why some parts of the world are more crowded than others

⊚ what geographers mean by 'settlement'

⊚ the kind of sites which encourage settlements to grow

⊚ the problems that occur when settlements grow very large.

World Population

Planet Earth, population 6 billion

Action needed now to avert disaster

Every day the world will gain another 230 000 people. Every week there is another Birmingham, every month another London and every year another Germany to feed, water and clothe.

Ninety-seven per cent of this population growth will take place in the developing world, where most people are already poor.

Good news

Population growth has peaked and is gradually slowing down

Bad news

Growth is not slowing down enough to secure good health for the poor. Their future remains bleak.

Cutting down the growth of the world's population will take time; 40 per cent of today's population are under 15 years of age. The parents of the next generation have already been born.

About 75 million pregnancies each year are unwanted. Between 120 and 150 million women who want to space their pregnancies cannot do so because they have no access to reliable family planning services.

In some ways, reaching 6 billion people is a triumph; it means that people are healthier and are living longer. People are not problems in themselves, but what they consume and how they share the Earth's resources could lead to very great problems that cannot be ignored.

A

Activities

1. Use table **B** to draw a graph to show the rise in world population.

2. From your graph, estimate the population in 2050 based on similar growth rates.

3. Read the following statements. With a partner, choose the best point on the graph for each one and add it as a label. Be careful – not all the statements are relevant!

   ⊚ Population reaches 1000 million.

   ⊚ Growth of population is at its slowest.

   ⊚ Getting crowded – 6 billion people in the world!

   ⊚ DANGER! Growth in the numbers of people out of control.

   ⊚ Phew! Some evidence of population growth slowing down.

   ⊚ Steady but constant rise in the world's population.

4. Write a paragraph to summarise what the graph tells you about the changes in world population since 1800.

5. Read these effects of population growth. Copy out the three that you think are the most important for the future of our planet. Give reasons for each choice.

   ⊚ There will be more elderly people in the world.

   ⊚ More people mean more mouths to feed.

   ⊚ If the world gets too crowded, there will be too little room for everybody.

   ⊚ More of the world's forests will be chopped down to provide the extra fuel needed.

   ⊚ There may be not enough clean water for everyone to use.

   ⊚ If there are more people, it is more likely that someone able to solve all the world's problems will be born.

   ⊚ There are already over a billion young people aged between 15 and 24 years.

6. **Extension**

   Look up http://www.y6b.org/ to find out more about the world's population. Select information to add to your answers to questions 1 to 5. **ICT**

The 6 billion milestone

On Tuesday 12 October 1999 the world's population was estimated to have reached 6 billion people. It took until 1804 for the population of our planet to reach 1 billion (that is, 1000 million) people, yet it took only 12 years for the population to increase from 5 billion to 6 billion.

Year	World population (millions)
1800	900
1850	1200
1900	1600
1930	2000
1950	2500
1960	3000
1970	3700
1980	4500
1990	5300
2000	6000

B How the world's population has changed since 1800

Why is the population of the world going up so much?

To understand this, you have to think of the population of a country as a system. Systems have inputs and outputs. If the input is larger than the output, the system will grow. If the output is greater than the input, the system will get smaller (see **A**).

To see why population increases at different rates throughout the world, you are going to look at two very different countries, Mali and the UK. Mali is a less economically developed country (**LEDC**). The UK is a more economically developed country (**MEDC**). Look at table **B**, which shows some basic differences.

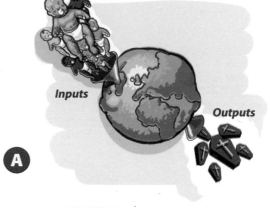

A

Country	UK	Mali
Birth rate	13	50
Death rate	11	20
Annual growth rate		
Infant mortality rate	6	134
Life expectancy (male / female)	74 / 79	44 / 48

B Population facts for UK and Mali

Activities

1. Copy out table **B**. Work out the figures for the annual growth rate (see Getting Technical) and add them to your table. (12)

2. Write a short paragraph to compare the population figures for the UK and Mali.

3. Suggest some extra information which might help you get a clearer picture of each country's population.

4. In pairs, choose one of the 'heads' below. Then choose one of the 'tails'. Write out the head and the tail, and then work out the result that goes with them. The first one has been done for you. Suggest as many heads and tails for each result as you can.

Heads	Tails	Results
High birth rate	High death rate	Population grows fast
Medium birth rate	Medium death rate	Population grows slowly
Low birth rate	Low death rate	Population stable
		Population goes down

High birth rate + Low death rate → Population grows fast

Getting Technical ▼

◎ **Birth rate**
The **birth rate** of a country is the average number of babies born to every 1000 people each year.

◎ **Death rate**
The **death rate** of a country is the average number of people who die for every 1000 people each year.

◎ **Annual growth rate**
Annual growth rate is found by taking away the death rate from the birth rate. It tells you how many extra people there are in a country per thousand each year. If the growth rate is large, the population is growing a lot. If it is a negative number, the population is actually going down each year. A country has a **stable population** when the death rate and birth rate are the same.

◎ **Infant mortality rate**
Infant mortality rate is a special type of death rate. It is the number of babies who die before their first birthday for every 1000 babies born.

◎ **Life expectancy**
Life expectancy is the average number of years that a person might expect to live. It gives a clue about the general health of a country's population.

◎ **Migration**
The population will change if people move either into or out of a country. When people move into a country it is called **immigration**. When people move out of a country it is called **emigration**.

Death rates have been going down all over the world

Death rates generally have been falling in most parts of the world over the past hundred years. There are a number of reasons for this.

Illnesses have been prevented because:

- more people have access to clean water
- more people enjoy a varied **diet**, which means better health
- pre-natal care for pregnant women is improving
- more babies are born in hospital, where expert help is on hand, rather than at home, especially in richer countries
- children are **inoculated** against killer diseases such as polio.

More ill people can be cured because of:

- better health facilities, such as clinics and hospitals
- better knowledge of disease.

Education and changes to our surroundings have helped as well, including:

- better health education
- better living conditions for some people
- more women in LEDCs receiving education
- in MEDCs, improved design for new housing and strict building regulations.

C Clean water helps people to stay healthy

Activities

1 Choose the one **factor** (reason) that you feel has been the most important in bringing down death rates. Discuss this with a partner. Give reasons for your choice.

2 Put the rest of the reasons in order of importance.

3 Start to make a word bank of key words for this unit.

   a Start with the words in **bold** on this page.

   b Add any key words you have learned from pages 44–46.

Birth rates are getting lower but are more difficult to reduce

Photographs **D** and **E** show two families in very different parts of the world. There are many reasons why couples have families of different sizes.

The role of children in MEDCs like the UK

In Britain, feeding, clothing and educating a child has cost its parents an average of over £50 000 by the time it is 17. Children can be seen as an **economic burden** to their parents.

⊚ *Schooling is compulsory; careers are specialised*

Nearly all young people go to school, but they cannot work full-time until they are 16. Most adults have a paid job, and some train for years for their career, so couples may not start a family until their late twenties or thirties. When children become adults and have careers of their own, they may move away from the region in which their parents live.

⊚ *Old people get pensions*

A well developed system of pensions and benefits means that few old people have to rely upon the income of their children.

⊚ *You don't have to get pregnant!*

Family planning is available in MEDCs, so couples can choose if and when to have children. Good health care means that most children are born healthy and survive childhood. Women in the UK have an average of only 1.7 children.

The role of children in LEDCs like Mali

In many communities, children contribute to the family income, so they are an **economic asset**. They often do jobs around the house or on the farm, such as collecting firewood or water. These jobs may take many hours and allow adults to do other tasks.

⊚ *Compulsory schooling is less widely available*

Education is often only provided at primary level, especially in the countryside. In Mali, only 31 per cent of children go to primary school.

⊚ *Elderly people rely on their children*

Many elderly people rely upon their children to look after them – children are seen as a form of security when there is no state pension.

⊚ *Many babies die in their first year*

High infant mortality rates can encourage couples to have lots of children; in Mali, the average family size is 6.7 children.

D A small family in the UK

Marcus and Cynthia Wright live in a small village in West Yorkshire, England. They both have professional jobs which take up a good deal of time. Marcus is a dentist and Cynthia is a barrister. Cynthia took maternity leave when she was 32 to have her first child, Jamie. Two years later Susie was born. Both parents juggle their time to manage their jobs and get the children to and from school and child-minders, as well as music, swimming and dancing lessons.

Fanta and Samba Coulibali live in Tomora, Mali, with their four children. A nephew also lives with them. They grow millet and struggle to find enough to eat every year. Even if the rains are good, their two small fields only give enough food for six months. This means that the family have to split up during part of the year to find food. Fanta often goes to the River Niger flood plain to help harvest rice. When they run out of food, they have to borrow sacks of millet, on which they have to pay interest.

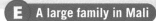

E **A large family in Mali**

Activities

1. Read about the roles of children in the UK and Mali. Make a copy of the grid below. Write notes about family size, education, health, children's work and benefits in the two countries. Make sure you include facts and figures.

	UK	Mali
Family size		
Education		
Health		
Children's work		
Benefits		

2. Read about the Wrights. Why do you think they have only two children?

3. Fanta and Samba Coulibali have a much larger family. Suggest reasons why this is so.

4. Use your work for questions **1–3** to write a short summary comparing families in the UK and Mali. First *describe* the main differences, then try to *explain* them.

5. How typical a UK family do you think the Wrights are? How typical are the Coulibalis? Discuss these questions with a partner, then describe what extra information you would need to find the answers.

6. Which of the two families puts more stress on the Earth's resources? Give reasons for your choice.

Population density

Population density is a measure of how many people live in an area of land. This is counted in people for each square kilometre (km^2). An area where many people live in a square kilometre has a *high population density*. In cities, population densities can be very high indeed: Hong Kong has a density of over 5000 people per km^2.

A Hong Kong has a high population density

Densities over larger areas, such as a country, are rarely as high as that. Any country with a population density of over 100 people per km^2 is said to have a high population density. The UK has a density of 244 people per km^2.

Areas where few people live per square kilometre have a *low population density* or are described as **sparsely populated**. Mali has a population density of 8 people per km^2. This is a sparsely populated country, even though there is a high rate of population growth.

There are a number of reasons or factors why some areas are more densely populated than others. Look back at the photograph of the Himalayas on page 44. It is not difficult to see why the population is sparse. A city like Rio de Janeiro (see page 70) has a very high population density, and it is easy to see why many people decided to live there.

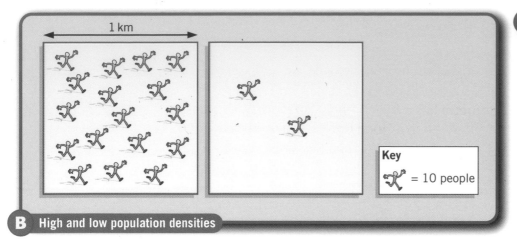

volcanic areas

good roads

steep slopes

foggy places

earthquake zones

high areas

lack of jobs

rich soil

rocky places

wet areas

thickly forested areas

good farming

very hot places

very cold places

temperate places

places likely to have blizzards

places with poor TV reception

coal-fields

coastal areas

river valleys

dry areas

difficult communications

industrial places

places likely to flood

sunny places

cloudy places

lowland areas

flat areas

places with many jobs

B High and low population densities

Key: 🏃 = 10 people

Activities

1 **a** Look at the boxes in **B**. Each one represents a square kilometre. Calculate the population density for each one.

   b Sketch copies of the boxes. Label them using the key words in bold from the text.

2 Think about the place that you live.

   a Does it have a high, medium or low population density?

   b List the factors in box **C** that describe where you live.

3 **a** Draw two spider diagrams, one for areas of high population density and one for areas of low density (sparse population). Link up each area with some of the factors from box **C**, as in the example below. Be careful – not all these factors may be relevant!

   b Work out which of your labels are to do with people (human factors). Colour code these red. Then work out which of your labels are natural (physical factors). Colour code these green.

   c Try to add to your diagrams by thinking of more factors.

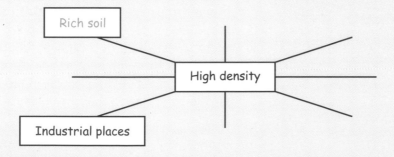

4 **Extension**

   ⑥ Try to split the physical and human factors on your diagrams into smaller categories (climate, **relief**, soils, vegetation, economic, social, etc.). Use a colour key to indicate these.

   ⑥ Find the places mentioned on pages 46–52 on a population density map in your atlas. How are high and low density areas shown on the map?

Case Study

Population distribution: Where do people live in Mali?

Geographers often ask these questions about the population in a country:

- Where in the country do most people live?

- Why do people live in these areas of high population density?

- Which areas are more sparsely populated? Why?

You have already seen that the population of Mali is increasing very rapidly (page 46). This is because of the high birth rate and the much lower death rate. Today Mali is one of the poorest countries in the world, although it has a proud history – Mali had a thriving and wealthy empire in the fourteenth century.

Much of Mali is in the Sahara desert. The desert has grown since the 1970s, and this has put more stress on the land. Most of the farmland is near the River Niger where the soil is fertile, but mosquitoes breed in swampy areas.

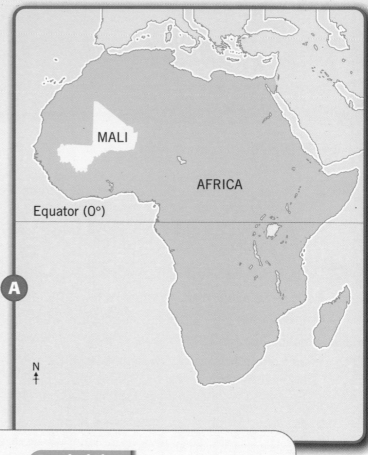

A

Equator (0°)

MALI

AFRICA

N ↑

Mali fact file

Land

- Land area is 1240 90 km².

- Sixty-five per cent is desert or semi-desert.

- The land north of 15 °N is true desert.

- In the south the land is over 1000 m above sea level.

People

- Total population is 9.9 million.

- Eighty per cent of the population work in farming or fishing.

- Ten per cent of the population are nomads who follow seasonal rains to find grass for their cattle.

Trade

- Mali is a land-locked country that relies on trade with the outside world.

- Cotton is an important export crop.

- Gold-mining has increased recently and gold could be a valuable export.

Activities

1. Read the information about Mali in the fact file and the text. Photos **C** and **D** may help, too. Make a copy of the table below and add factors (reasons) for a high population density or for a low population density in different parts of the country. Take care – not all the information may be relevant!

Factors affecting population density in Mali

Factors encouraging a high population density	Factors encouraging a low population density

2. Look again at your table. Overall, do you think Mali's population density will be high, medium or low? Explain why you think so.

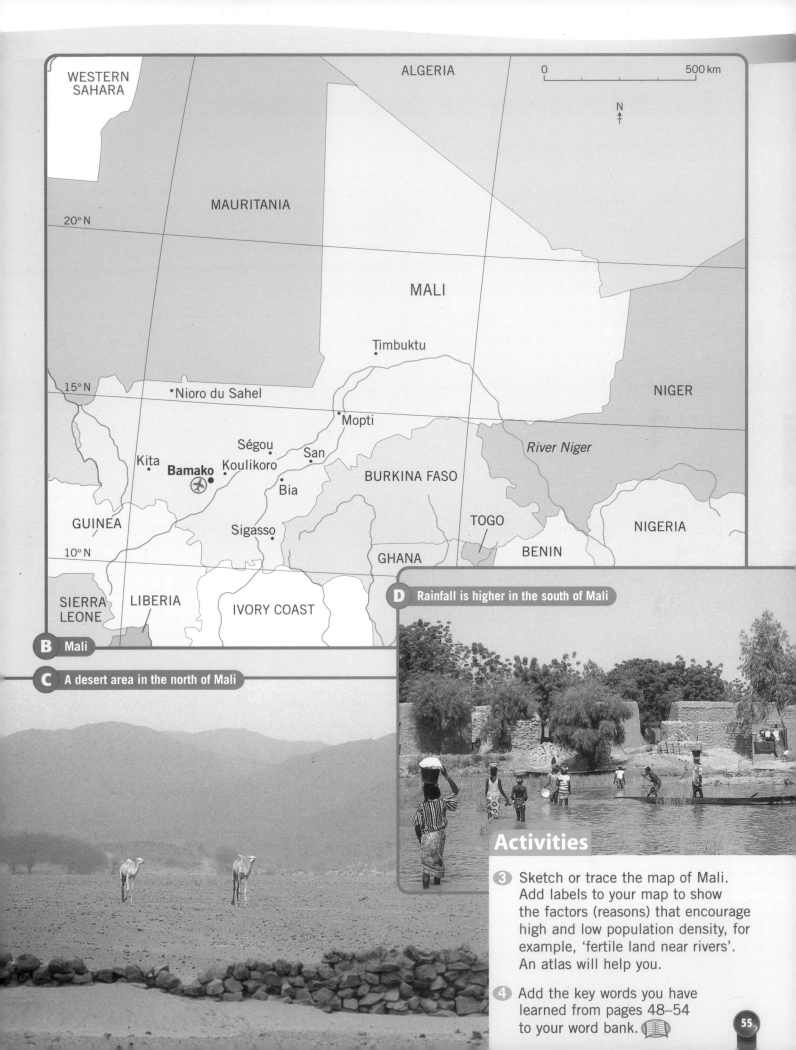

WESTERN
SAHARA

ALGERIA

0   500 km

N

MAURITANIA

20° N

MALI

Timbuktu

15° N   •Nioro du Sahel

NIGER

•Mopti

Ségou   River Niger

Kita   •   •   •San
      Bamako •Koulikoro
        ✈   •Bia

BURKINA FASO

GUINEA   TOGO   NIGERIA

10° N

Sigasso •   BENIN

GHANA

SIERRA   LIBERIA
LEONE   IVORY COAST

D Rainfall is higher in the south of Mali

B Mali

C A desert area in the north of Mali

Activities

3 Sketch or trace the map of Mali.
Add labels to your map to show
the factors (reasons) that encourage
high and low population density, for
example, 'fertile land near rivers'.
An atlas will help you.

4 Add the key words you have
learned from pages 48–54
to your word bank. 📖

Distribution of population: looking globally

Study map **A** closely, taking time to look at the population density in each of the seven continents throughout the world. The density of some continents is easy to describe and give reasons for. For example, Antarctica is the only continent with no permanent population. It is easy to explain why this is so (see page 53 if you need help on this). The pattern in other continents is more complicated. The pictures on this page and pages 44, 52 and 55 show some of the reasons why some parts of the world are sparsely populated and others have high population densities.

A World population distribution

NORTH AMERICA

EUROPE

ASIA

Equator

AFRICA

SOUTH AMERICA

OCEANIA

Key
Density of population, 1997

- over 100 people per km²
- 10–100 people per km²
- under 10 people per km²

ANTARCTICA

B Antarctica is the least populated continent

C Bangladesh has a population density of about 950 people per km²

D Sydney, Australia, has a high population density, although overall Australia has a population of less than 10 people per km²

E The Nevada desert, in the United States, is sparsely populated

Population record-breakers

- The world's fastest growing countries are Kuwait, Namibia, Afghanistan, Mali and Tanzania.

- The world's slowest growing countries are Belgium, Hungary, Grenada, Germany and Tonga.

- The two countries with the largest populations are China and India.

- Tristan da Cunha and the Pitcairn Islands have the smallest populations.

- Macau has a population density of over 22 000 people per km².

- Greenland has only 0.2 people per km².

Review and reflect

In this unit you have learned about population distribution and growth. Your final assignment is to produce a poster summarising what you have learned about population. Use the steps below to help you focus your ideas. Your teacher may ask you to work in a group for this assignment.

1. Start with an atlas map showing world population distribution. Label the main areas of high population density. Give some reasons for this density. The photographs on this page and on page 56 may help.

2. Label two or more countries where the population is growing fast, and some countries where it is growing slowly.

3. Label two countries that have very different population structures. Add sketches of their population pyramids to your poster. Add some labels to explain what the pyramids tell you about the two countries.

4. Finally, discuss why the world's population is an important issue and some of the ways in which the population crisis could be lessened. Choose three or more ideas from box **F** and explain how each one would help. Add your work to the poster; you may be able to suggest where in the world your solutions would work best.

- Education
- Providing better water
- Conserving the resources of the Earth
- More reliable methods of contraception
- Using less fossil fuel
- Improving opportunities for women
- Tree-planting schemes
- Introducing better types of crops
- **Irrigating** the deserts
- Building into the sea
- Launching people into space to colonise other planets.

F Ways of lessening the population crisis

What is a settlement?

A settlement is a place where people live. Geographers are often interested in how many people live within a particular area (*settlement size* or *type*), the exact location of the settlement (*settlement site*) and what goes on in the settlement (*settlement function*).

You are going to look at the answers to these three enquiry questions:

- ⑥ What is a settlement?
- ⑥ Where do people build settlements?
- ⑥ Why do they choose those places to build settlements?

Where do you live?

Most people, if asked this very basic question, would reply that they lived in a house. Some people might name the place or the road. Most people live in one place throughout the year, and are said to live in a **permanent settlement**. A few people might have difficulty in giving a straightforward answer: they may live in a **temporary settlement** and move from place to place.

Activities

1. For each photograph, decide whether it shows a permanent or a temporary settlement. Give reasons for your choice.

2. Construct a brainstorm diagram. Show as many reasons as you can why people might live in temporary settlements.

3. Colour those reasons why people are *forced* to live in a temporary settlement in red. Use blue to show the reasons why people *choose* to do so.

4. **Extension**
   Research and collect more photographs that show settlements.
   Comment on each photograph in the same way that you did in question **1**.

hint

Be careful, some photographs may not show a settlement at all! There may be no simple answer for some of the others. It all depends upon the reasons you give.

Settlement sites

The exact position that a settlement occupies is often called its **site**.
Many settlements have very useful sites that have encouraged the
settlements to grow. Look at these descriptions of good settlement sites.

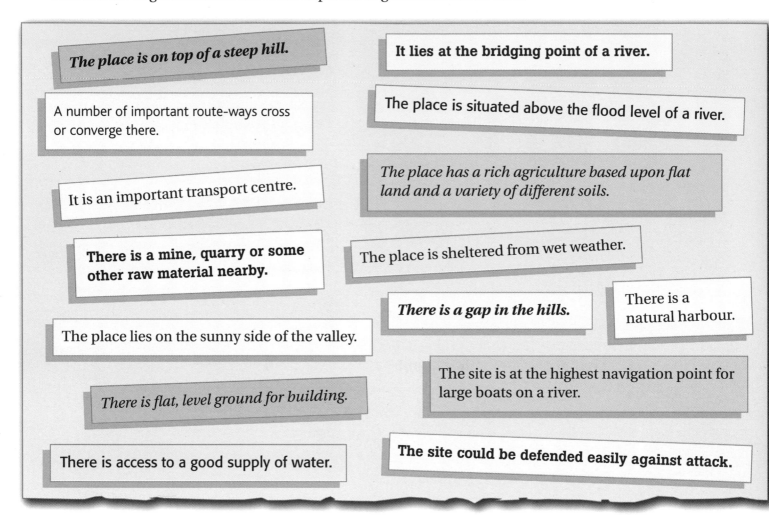

The place is on top of a steep hill.

It lies at the bridging point of a river.

A number of important route-ways cross or converge there.

The place is situated above the flood level of a river.

It is an important transport centre.

The place has a rich agriculture based upon flat land and a variety of different soils.

There is a mine, quarry or some other raw material nearby.

The place is sheltered from wet weather.

There is a gap in the hills.

There is a natural harbour.

The place lies on the sunny side of the valley.

The site is at the highest navigation point for large boats on a river.

There is flat, level ground for building.

There is access to a good supply of water.

The site could be defended easily against attack.

The site of a settlement is not necessarily good; this may mean that
the settlement does not grow as fast as those with more successful
sites. Here are some examples of sites that are not very good.

There is little flat land.

The settlement can't expand because of a major road.

There is flooding from a river or the sea.

The roads have become very congested because they are too narrow.

Important roads no longer pass through the settlement.

The original reason for its existence has now gone.

Settlement along the River Severn

The River Severn is the UK's longest river. It flows from Wales through parts of England and runs into the Bristol Channel. Until the railways were built in the mid 1800s, it was much easier to carry people and goods by boat than over the land, so many people settled near rivers like the Severn. Look carefully at the map on this page. It shows the course of the river and the sites of many settlements along it. Then look at the information about some of these sites on pages 62–66 before you do the activity on page 67.

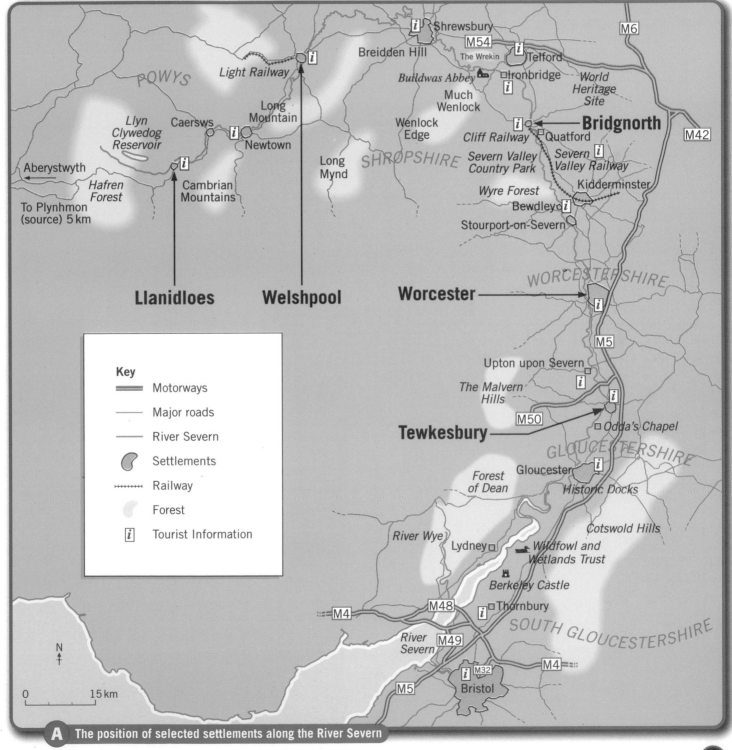

A The position of selected settlements along the River Severn

Tewkesbury

Tewkesbury has a long street which is lined with ancient buildings, including the Abbey. It is sited on the eastern side of the River Severn at its **confluence** (joining place) with the River Avon.

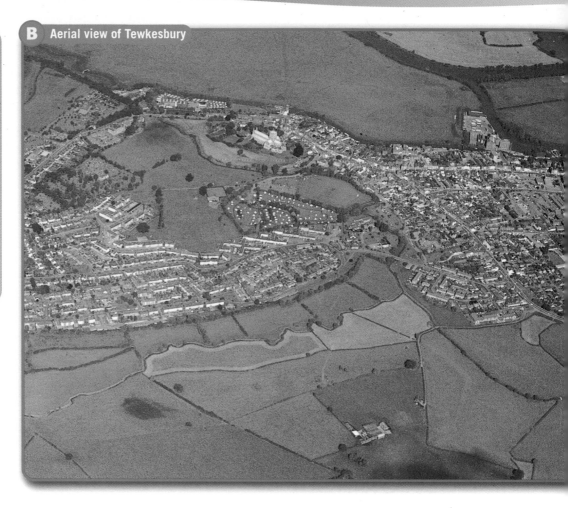

B Aerial view of Tewkesbury

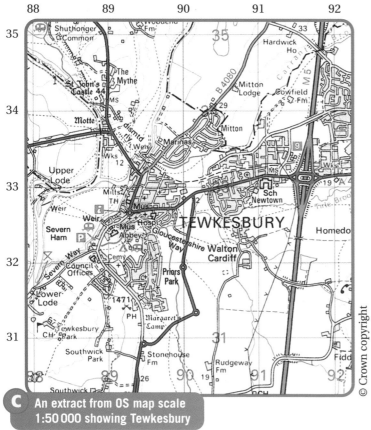

C An extract from OS map scale 1:50 000 showing Tewkesbury

© Crown copyright

D Tewkesbury

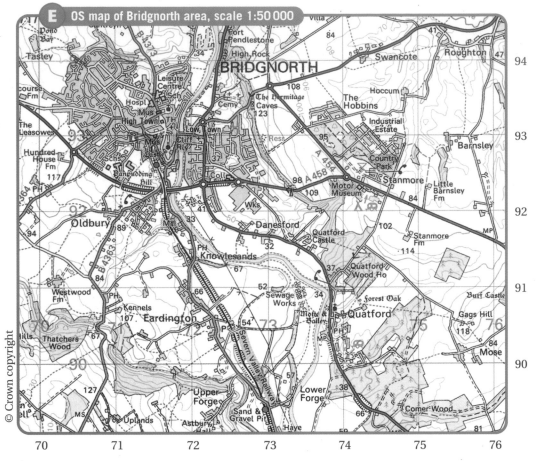

E OS map of Bridgnorth area, scale 1:50 000

Bridgnorth

The lower part of the town, or Low Town, lies either side of the magnificent River Severn, while the higher part, or High Town, is perched on dramatic sandstone cliffs 30 metres high. The two parts of the town are linked by historic winding steps and a unique cliff railway.

There is so much to see, both in the town itself and in the surrounding area, that visitors are well advised to allow plenty of time for their visit to this ancient market town!

F Aerial view of Bridgnorth

Llanidloes

Llanidloes is a historic market town in the centre of Wales. It lies at the confluence (joining place) of the rivers Clywedog and Severn. There are two bridges over the Severn in the town. The main A470(T) bypasses the town on the south-east. The site of the town is restricted on the north and north-west by steep slopes. The Tudor market hall in the picture is now a museum. There are many other interesting buildings from Tudor, Georgian and Victorian times.

G The market hall in Llanidloes was built in Tudor times

H OS map of Llanidloes, scale 1:50 000

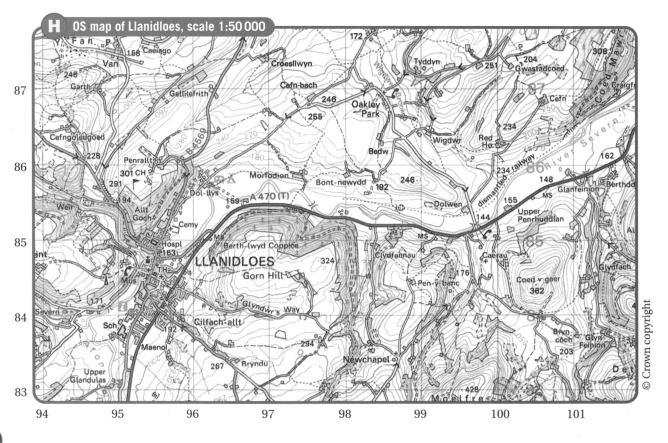

© Crown copyright

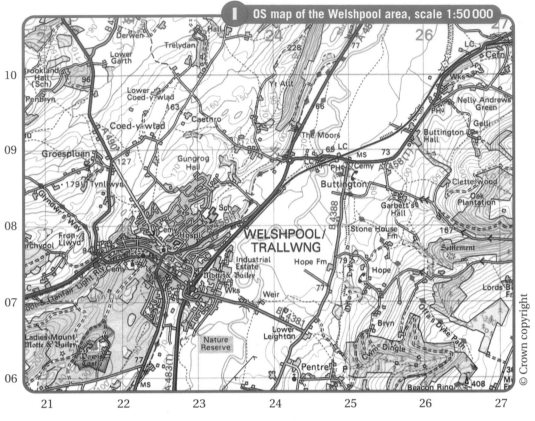

I OS map of the Welshpool area, scale 1:50 000

© Crown copyright

Welshpool

Welshpool is a busy market town in Mid Wales. Bronze Age remains have been found nearby, and it was a civilian settlement in Roman times. Medieval Powis Castle, 1.5 km south of the town, is perched on a rock with terraced gardens below.

J The main street in Welshpool attracts shoppers from the surrounding countryside

Historic Worcester

The city of Worcester is situated on the River Severn, the longest river in Britain. The original settlement was sited on the east bank of the river but today Worcester has grown into a city of 90,000 people.

The battle of Worcester in 1651, when Oliver Cromwell defeated Prince Charles, marked the end of the Civil War in England. It earned Worcester the name "The Faithful City" for its Royalist support.

Worcester is home to Royal Worcester Porcelain and the famous 'Worcester Sauce', and it is the birthplace of the British composer, Sir Edward Elgar.

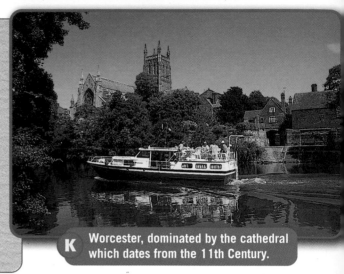

K Worcester, dominated by the cathedral which dates from the 11th Century.

© Crown copyright

L OS map of the Worcester area, scale 1:50 000

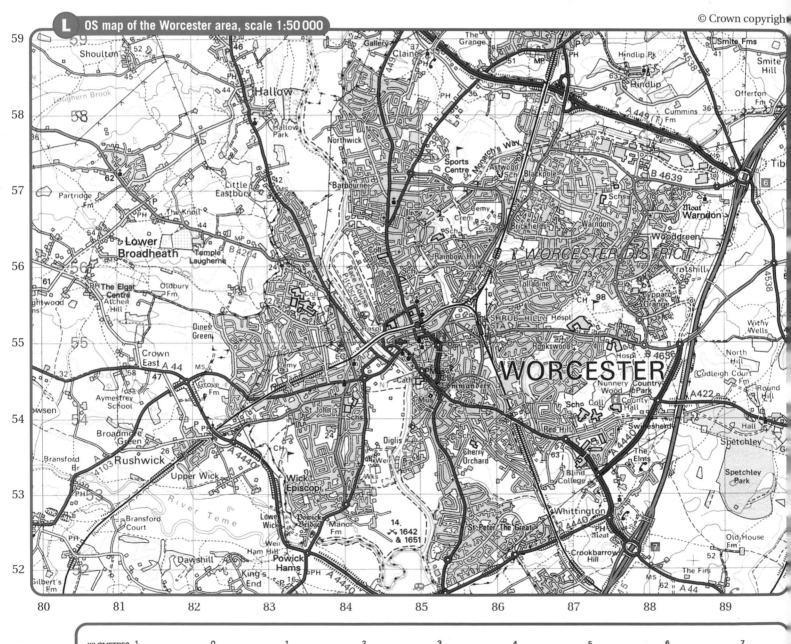

KILOMETRES

M Scale bar for 1:50 000 scale maps

Activities

1. Look back at map **A** on page 61 and the other information for the sample settlements on the River Severn. For each settlement, use clues from the maps, photos and text to try to analyse its site. You might like to set your work for each settlement out like this:

Settlement name	Bridgnorth
Settlement type	[city, regional centre, market town, etc.] Market town
Location	
Site description	Bridgnorth is sited on a steep hill ... It is a defensive site because ... and ...
Good things about its site	Bridging point of river; main town doesn't flood; ...
Bad things about its site	Steep slopes; little space for expansion except on the flood plain; ...
Your verdict	Give the settlement site a mark out of 10. 5/10
Reasons for your verdict	It is an important bridging point, but defence is no longer important and the town can't expand ...
Special features of the settlement	It could be an important tourist place, because it has a castle, so it may be a good thing that it can't expand much ...

2. Use the scale to estimate the size of each settlement you have studied. Find the size of the settlement in kilometres from north to south and west to east. ⒈②③

3. Make a display of your work by organising your notes on each settlement around a large copy of map **A** on page 61.

4. Add words you have learned about settlement to your word bank. 📖

5. **Extension**
   Study the 1:50 000 OS map of the area where you live. Analyse the sites of four or five different settlements. How do they compare with those in the Severn Valley?

The living city

In this section, you are going to investigate a much larger settlement. Rio de Janeiro, in South America, is a very large city in a part of the world very different from the Severn Valley. After investigating this city, you should have the skills to enquire into another city anywhere in the world. For any city, try to investigate:

⑥ the location of the city

⑥ what different parts of the city are like

⑥ why there are differences between the different parts of the city

⑥ what changes are taking place within the settlement

⑥ how people are trying to improve the environments in which they live.

Investigating Rio de Janeiro

The first stage in this geographical investigation or **enquiry** is to make sure you understand clearly the location of this settlement. Geographers describe a settlement's location in two ways that are at two different scales.

The site of a settlement means its detailed location, so this is on a small scale. When geographers describe the site, they often look at the physical features of the place it is built on. Descriptions of settlement sites often include:

⑥ details of relief features, like hills and valleys

⑥ the site's access to water, for example rivers or springs

⑥ other details like soil type, vegetation and local climate.

Some of this information might be difficult to find out without fieldwork.

The **situation** of a settlement looks at the broader picture of where a place is located. Geographers often describe the situation of a place by linking its location to that of other places. The situation of a settlement can be described by looking at an atlas.

help!

Atlas entries are sometimes listed like this:

Wolverhampton	5	D4	52°N	2°W
place or feature	page	grid square	latitude	longitude

Activities

① Use your atlas to locate the city of Rio de Janeiro. Look up the entry in the index of your atlas and write that down exactly.

② Using the index entry, write a few sentences to describe how it helps you to find where the city is on one of the atlas maps. You could use your own words or set it out like this:

> Rio de Janeiro is at latitude ____ °S and longitude ____ °W. It is found on page ____ of my atlas. It is in the grid square ____. The city is in the country of ____...

③ a Use the index entry to find Rio de Janeiro in the atlas. Draw a quick sketch map to show its situation within the continent of South America and the country of Brazil.

b Write two sentences which describe the situation of Rio. Label these onto your sketch map.

④ Look at the picture and the detailed map of Rio de Janeiro. Write a description of the site of the city.

Setting the scene – what is Rio like?

Rio de Janeiro is a very large city of 11 million people. Sometimes said to be the most beautiful and liveliest of all cities, it is famous for its carnival, its samba (a dance) and its natural beauty. It is sited to the west of a magnificent bay, with the dazzling beaches of Ipanema and Copacabana on one side and a forest-covered mountain range on the other.

Rio de Janeiro has two very famous landmarks: the Sugar Loaf Mountain, and a statue called 'Christ the Redeemer'. This statue is sited at the top of Corcovado Mountain, and can be seen for miles around. The map and photographs give some idea what the city is like.

A **Rio carnival**

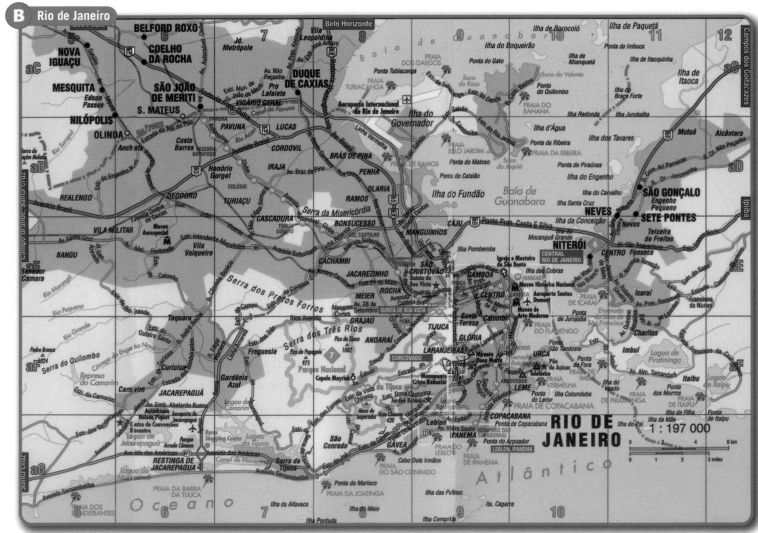

B **Rio de Janeiro**

C Aerial view of Rio de Janeiro

The city centre (or Downtown Rio)

D Downtown Rio

It is difficult to say exactly where the centre of Rio is, because the city is so huge. Slopes and steep mountains rise up so suddenly from the coastline that flat land is in short supply, so the city centre is broken up into many different sections. Tunnels have been cut into the hillsides to connect one part of the city centre with another. The **Central Business District (CBD)** is the area where many shops and offices are located. The old historical centre is also in this part of the city.

The glamorous central part of Rio is busy 24 hours a day. There are busy streets, hectic noise and chaotic traffic. There are expensive shopping areas and constant street trading. Only rich people can afford to live in apartments in this area. Many of the high-rise buildings are part of the financial centre where large firms have their South American and Brazilian headquarters.

Activities

5 Write a detailed paragraph to summarise what the centre of Rio is like. Use drawings, cartoons and maps to make your descriptive work really full.

6 Write a second paragraph about the city centre to explain why this area is like it is. You may be able to suggest what changes you think may occur in this part of the city, and the reasons.

help! ICT

Use ICT to add to your description of the city centre.

☼ Start by looking at CD-ROM encyclopaedias. Remember to edit text before you use it.

☼ Extend your investigation by searching the Internet. http://www.ipanema.com and http://www.bondinho.com.br may give useful results. Use a search engine to make your own enquiry.

Contrasts within the city

It is easy to see the glamour of Rio de Janeiro, especially along the beaches of Copacabana and Ipanema. But there is a darker side to the city. There is great economic hardship for some of the residents. Not far from the beaches you can see serious crime, such as drug-trafficking, and problems in policing. Above all, there is a tremendous strain on the city authorities to provide services for everyone.

You are going to look at three different parts of the city. Many of the poor areas are made up of informal housing or **shanty towns**, called *favelas* in South America.

Rocinha

Rocinha is one of the largest *favelas* in Rio de Janeiro, with about 100 000 people. It is like a big town within the city. Although it is built on steep slopes overlooking Copacabana beach, it is not on the main tourist trail. It is an area of **self-build housing**.

E Rocinha

The first residents of this huge *favela* came from the Brazilian countryside 40 years ago to find a better life in the city. A city like Rio thrives on cheap **labour**. Some people work in the factories around Rio's port. Others make a living from offering services around the city, such as selling food, working in bars, cleaning for better-off families, security work or fetching and carrying goods. Many of these jobs are **informal** and may be poorly paid.

When Rocinha was a new settlement, it was made up of wooden shacks. These were often perched unsafely on the steep slopes found all over the city. Now things are different. The houses are mainly built of brick and have rooms with balconies. There are basic services such as electricity, rubbish collection, street-lighting, running water and sewage disposal. Often these services were organised by the residents themselves: they did not wait for the city authorities to act.

Despite the community spirit within the *favelas*, they are still tough places to live. Their crime rates are often unacceptably high. However, by doing well at school, young people can try to escape the poverty of the *favelas*. It is difficult to take a vehicle into Rocinha because of the narrow streets and steep slopes, so its relatively central location is very important to the people.

Barra da Tijuca

The new 'city' of Barra da Tijuca is 10 km west of the edge of Rio. Barra is on the coast, where there is a lagoon of shallow water and flat land, so it has room to expand, unlike Rio which is hemmed in by mountains.

Barra has a population of 150 000. Many people live in high-rise apartments with high security, and there are excellent services, for example shopping malls along the dual carriageways. The beach at Barra is less crowded and more exclusive than those nearer to the city centre. Many of Rio's professional people are leaving the city to live in places on the outskirts like Barra. They can commute back on the motorway to the city centre if they need to, while enjoying the safer, quieter and more exclusive living conditions. Barra has grown very quickly and has been planned in a rather haphazard way. The number of people wanting to escape the chaos of central Rio has put great pressure on this new settlement.

F Barra da Tijuca

The area of newest arrivals on the edge of the city

The city's population is not growing any more, but people are still moving into the city. The **out-migration** of middle-class people is balanced by **in-migration** of the very poorest people in Brazil. The causes for this migration are common to many less economically developed countries.

Many poor Brazilians from the countryside struggle to earn a living. They have moved in search of a better life, often to a city or large town. Cities like Rio cannot cope with the im-migration of many very poor people, so these people are forced to fend for themselves. They may occupy land illegally and create *favelas* in places that are not ideal for safe building. The only available space is often the edge of the city, on steeply sloping areas or in areas which may flood (see **G**).

G Favela built on Rio's steep slopes

Activities

7 Use the headings in the help box to describe and explain the three different areas of Rio and its surroundings:

⊚ Barra   ⊚ Rocinha (an established *favela*)

⊚ The area of the newest arrivals to the city (unimproved *favelas*).

a *Describe* what each area is like and the kind of lives that people who live there might lead.

b *Explain* why the area is like it is and how it might change in the future.

help!

Include information about the location, the physical geography of the area, the jobs people do, the type of housing, and the services offered. Add detail by searching the Internet, as you did for the city centre. **ICT**

Activities

8 Your final task is to produce a labelled poster to summarise the contrasts in the city of Rio. You may be asked to work in a pair or a group for this activity.

   a Draw a sketch map of the city. Label the city centre, Rocinha, Barra da Tijuca and the latest developments on the outskirts of Rio.

   b Present the most important parts from your answers to **5**, **6** and **7** as bullet points. Try to show the main changes in each area. Remember that the poster is about *contrasts* within the city. Include illustrations from a number of sources.

9 **Extension**
Make a presentation to show how the parts of your poster are linked to each other. It may help to use another colour for this. Think about the movement of people throughout the city every day, as well as long-term migrations, and about different types of jobs in the city, for example formal and informal work.

Review and reflect

Summary of the Rio de Janeiro investigation

	Page
Ⓖ Geographers often start their investigations into places by locating them. You found out the **situation** of Rio by using an atlas.	68
Ⓖ More detailed maps and photographs of the city showed you the **site** of the settlement, the place where it is built.	69–70
Ⓖ Like many towns and cities, Rio has a central area which geographers call the **central business district**.	70
Ⓖ Outside the centre of the city, there are great contrasts between different neighbourhoods. In cities like Rio the pressure for housing is often so great that people are forced to build their own houses.	71–72

In time, some areas of self-build housing, or **favelas**, are improved. But on the edge of the city, new arrivals have to find a home.

Activities

Look back at your work on Rio de Janeiro using the page numbers in the summary table above to help.

1 In pairs, test that you understand what the key words (in bold) mean. For each word, try to think of another place where you can describe an example. 📖

2 Discuss what was the most interesting thing you found out, a new skill you learned and something you need to improve upon.

4 Flood disaster

How do people cope?

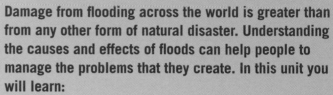

Learn about

Damage from flooding across the world is greater than from any other form of natural disaster. Understanding the causes and effects of floods can help people to manage the problems that they create. In this unit you will learn:

⊚ what happens to water when it lands on the ground

⊚ what causes floods

⊚ how people respond to floods

⊚ how the effects of flooding in the United Kingdom are different from those in Mozambique.

A

In February 2000, Mozambique, a country in south-east Africa, suffered devastating flooding. Look carefully at photograph **A** on the opposite page. The dry land around the base of the tree is keeping a family safe from the flooded rivers.

Activities

1 Work in pairs to answer the following questions.

a Who do you think took this photograph?

b What might the view from the top of the tree look like?

c How many people are on the dry land in the photograph?

d How big do you think the piece of dry land is?

e Name five things, other than people, that are on the dry land.

f Why do you think these things were important enough for the family to save?

g Name three things in the tree.

h Why do you think they have put these things in the tree?

i What other things, that cannot be seen, will the family need to survive?

j Where will they go to the toilet?

k Why might this cause problems?

l Is the weather warm or cold?

m What is the evidence for this?

n What shelter does the family have?

o Why might this be a problem?

p Why might these people be waiting, rather than trying to escape?

q Who might rescue them, and how?

2 Do you think Mozambique is a rich or a poor country?

3 What impact will this have on how Mozambique copes with flooding?

In 1998 large areas of the United Kingdom were affected by flooding. Over the Easter holiday, flooding caused damage worth £400 million, five people died and more than 1500 people were **evacuated** from their homes. Then, in October 1998, about 8000 square kilometres of England and Wales were flooded. The River Wye was 5 metres above its winter level and more than 160 kilometres of the River Severn were on red flood warning alert (see page 80 for a definition). Two thousand homes were cut off by flood water for two days.

B

Activities

4 Using the questions in activity **1** above to help you, write down five geographical questions you could ask someone about photograph **B**. Your questions should try to make that person think carefully about how flooding affects people's lives, and how the people might feel about it.

5 Swap questions with another person. Answer each other's questions.

6 In a pair, compare your questions and decide on the best five. Write down what you think makes a good geographical question.

7 The United Kingdom is a much richer country than Mozambique. How will this affect the ways in which it copes with flooding?

Understanding flooding: what happens to water when it reaches the ground?

Water lands on the Earth's surface as **precipitation**. Precipitation is part of a never-ending process called the **water cycle**. The simplified version of the water cycle in figure **A** shows how water **evaporates** from the sea and land, rises and **condenses** to form clouds. It then falls back to Earth as precipitation. To understand how flooding is caused it is important to know what happens to water when it reaches the ground. When precipitation lands on the Earth's surface it will either:

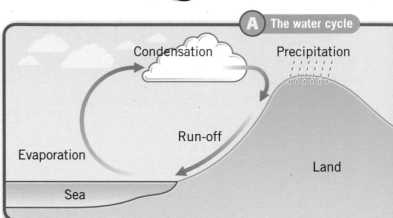

A The water cycle

- **infiltrate** (sink in) and flow as **groundwater** into rivers or be used and **transpired** by plants

- lie on the ground surface and eventually **evaporate**

- flow over the surface of the ground as **surface run-off**.

Whether or not the water infiltrates depends on many different factors, such as:

- if the ground is **permeable** or **impermeable**

- if the ground is flat or sloping

- how heavily the rain is falling.

Water which flows over the land as surface run-off tends to reach rivers much more quickly than groundwater.

Getting Technical ▾

Precipitation
Water falling from the air to Earth as rain, hail, sleet or snow.

Evaporation
The change of water from a liquid, which is visible, to water vapour, which is an invisible gas.

Transpiration
Water vapour given off by plants into the air.

Condensation
The change of invisible water vapour in the air into liquid droplets which are visible as cloud.

Surface run-off
The flow of water over the ground surface, including rivers and streams.

Groundwater flow
The flow of water beneath the ground surface. The water has to seep between the air spaces in soil and rocks, which makes it slower than surface run-off.

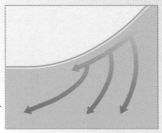

Infiltration
When water sinks into the ground.

Permeable
Ground that allows water to pass through it.

Impermeable
Ground that does not allow water to pass through it.

Activity

Fieldwork enquiry
Asking questions

You are going to investigate one big enquiry question:

> **What happens to water when it reaches the ground?**

1 You must answer some geographical questions by carrying out a piece of fieldwork in your school grounds.

What happens to water when:

a it lands on a flat surface?

b it lands on a sloping surface?

c it lands on a permeable surface such as grass or soil?

d it lands on an impermeable surface such as concrete or tarmac?

e it falls quickly or heavily?

f it falls slowly or gently?

2 Collecting information

a Go out into your school grounds with a watering-can full of water and carry out research into questions **1a–f** above. Observe the water landing on different types of surface at different rates (heavily and gently). Record exactly what happens each time using words from the Getting Technical box.

b When you get back to the classroom, write the title:

What happens to water when it reaches the ground?

Then write the side-heading *Method* and describe exactly what you did in order to research the enquiry questions.

3 Presenting your results

a Design a table to show your results. Include drawings that show clearly what happened at each place where you poured the water.

b Find a way to show the results on a map of your school.

4 Describing and explaining your results

Write the side-heading *Conclusions*. For each of the six questions **1a–f** above, describe what happened and give as many reasons for this as you can. You *must* use the following words in your answers:

infiltrate   permeable   impermeable   surface run-off

5 Predict what will happen to water when:

a it lands on steeply sloping permeable ground

b it falls very gently onto flat impermeable ground

c it falls quickly onto flat permeable ground.

6 Suggest three more geographical questions about 'What happens to water when it reaches the ground?' that you could have investigated.

7 How does knowing about what happens to water when it reaches the ground help people to understand why rivers flood? Try to include something about *infiltration, permeable* and *impermeable ground, surface run-off, groundwater flow* and *transpiration*.

What causes the River Severn in the United Kingdom to flood?

A River Severn flooding west of Shrewsbury in 1998

The town of Shrewsbury is built on the banks of the River Severn in Shropshire. The Ordnance Survey map on page 81 shows you the location of Shrewsbury.

At the end of October 1998 the River Severn flooded parts of Shrewsbury and the surrounding area twice in one week. A river flood happens when there is too much water for the river channel to hold. This causes the water in the channel to overflow and cover the nearby land. The River Severn often floods and is famous for how quickly its water level rises and falls. For example, the great flood of 1795 destroyed most of the bridges on the Severn, sixteen of them in Shropshire. River flooding along the Severn is caused by a combination of physical and human factors.

Factors that cause the River Severn to flood

The amount of precipitation

The area of Wales where the River Severn has its source has a large amount of precipitation. This means that there is a lot of water to drain away in rivers. The month of October 1998 was one of the wettest ever recorded – 135 mm of rain fell, twice as much as usual. The ground in the drainage basin was already very wet. On 22 October heavy rain storms added to the problem – the ground could not absorb any more water.

The size of the drainage basin

The area of land drained by a river is called its **drainage basin**. The River Severn's drainage basin is 11 400 km^2 – the largest in England and Wales. This means it has to drain more precipitation away than smaller basins.

The steepness of the slopes

The River Severn begins its journey to the sea in the mountains of Wales. A lot of the land here is very steep, so precipitation flows quickly into the river.

The type of vegetation (plants)

Most of the River Severn's drainage basin is covered by moorland and grassland. This type of **vegetation** does not use up and transpire as much water as trees. Although the basin was once covered in woodland, people have cut down most of the trees to make space for farming.

The number of tributaries

The higher the number and the greater the size of the **tributaries** in a drainage basin, the quicker the water will reach the main river. The River Severn has twelve large tributaries, increasing the risk of flooding downstream from them.

Building towns and cities

The River Severn has many towns and cities along its course, such as Shrewsbury, Bridgnorth and Bewdley (see map **A** on page 61). In these built-up areas, impermeable surfaces increase the risk of flooding because they cause surface run-off, which reaches the river quickly. Impermeable surfaces can also stop flood water from infiltrating so that the flooding lasts longer.

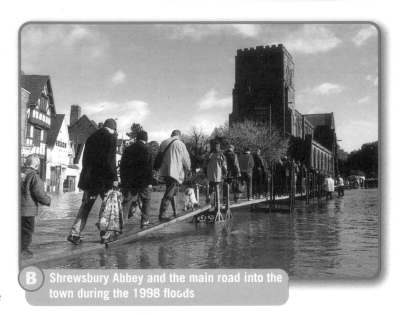

B Shrewsbury Abbey and the main road into the town during the 1998 floods

Activities

1. What is a river flood?

2. Copy the table below. Write each of the physical and human causes of flooding for the River Severn into the correct column.

Physical causes	Human causes

WHERE THE WASH-OUT IS WORST

MELVERLEY: Severe flooding. Homes abandoned

SHREWSBURY: Worst flooding for more than 30 years with over 200 homes affected

RIVERS WYE /ARROW: About 2000 homes in this area cut off for two days

BRIDGNORTH: Homes flooded

HEREFORD: Roughly 100 properties affected this week

BEWDLEY: Twenty people evacuated. Residents report worst flooding since 1947

ROSS-ON-WYE: More than 30 properties flooded, including old cattle market

Key
● Towns flooded
○ Towns under threat

0   20 km

C Places affected when the River Severn flooded in 1998, adapted from the *Sunday Telegraph*

3. Use map **C** from the *Sunday Telegraph* newspaper to name five of the River Severn's tributaries.

4. Which of these tributaries joins the River Severn before it reaches Shrewsbury?

5. Name the four towns on the Severn affected by flooding.

6. According to the *Sunday Telegraph*, at least how many properties (including homes) were affected by the floods?

7. Study photograph **A**. How do you think people living in this area will be affected by floods? Make five suggestions.

What are the effects of the River Severn flooding?

Activities

Getting to know the area on the map

1 The River Severn flows from west to east on the map. Follow the course of the river with your finger from where it appears on the map to where it leaves the map.

   a Is the name of the last village you go past Montford or Emstrey?

   b How many road bridges cross the River Severn on the map?

   c What other type of bridge crosses the River Severn?

   d Which road crosses the River Severn at both grid references 429152 and 522109?

2 The distance along the River Severn between grid references 429152 and 522109 is 40 km.

   a What is the straight line distance in kilometres?

   b How many times longer is the distance along the river than the straight line distance?

   c What does this tell you about the course of the River Severn?

Disaster at Montford Bridge, October 1998

3 **a** *Thursday 22 October: Environment Agency puts Shrewsbury on a red flood warning alert.* What does this mean?

   b *Friday 23 October: At Preston Montford (grid reference 4314) 42 mm of rain has fallen in 24 hours.* Is Preston Montford north, south, east or west of Shrewsbury?

   c *Monday 26 October: The River Severn has flooded many areas of Shrewsbury. Welsh Bridge (grid reference 488127) and English Bridge (grid reference 496124) are closed. The Toll bridge between these bridges is still open.* What is the six-figure grid reference for the Toll bridge?

Environment Agency – Levels of flood warning

Yellow Warning: flooding to roads and low-lying land from wind-blown spray.

Amber Warning: flooding to isolated properties, roads and large areas of farmland near rivers.

Red Warning: serious flooding affecting many properties, roads and areas of farmland near rivers.

   d *10.00 a.m. Wednesday 28 October: A phone call tells Shropshire fire and rescue service that fallen trees have jammed under the bridge at Montford Bridge. The rising water behind the bridge could destroy it, sending a wave of flood water down the valley.* What problems could this disaster cause in grid square 4315?

   e *The fire service's heavy lifting gear can only be moved along A and B roads.* What colours are A and B roads on the OS map?

   f *The fire station is at grid reference 496135. The rescue team must reach Montford Bridge quickly to save the bridge.* Work out the best route for the fire engine to take.

Don't forget that some bridges are closed.

   g Write down directions from the fire station to Montford Bridge. Include the numbers of the roads the fire engine should follow and the compass direction it should travel in on each road. Include ten places or features the fire engine will go through or past.

KEY

Bridge	Road bridge
Railway	Railway bridge
A 572	Dual carriageway
B 5204	A road
PH Public House	B road
X Camp site	Church
Caravan site	Contour

0   1 km
2 cm

How do people respond to floods in the United Kingdom?

Activities

1. Use a long ruler to measure a depth of 60 cm. Imagine that your home gets flooded with water this deep.

   a Make a list of all the damage and problems that might be caused by the water, both inside and outside your home.

   b If the flooding in your local area lasts for a week, what further problems might be created for you and the rest of your family? Add these to your list.

   c List all the things your family could have done, or could do, to reduce the damage and problems caused by the flood.

   d List other people or organisations that might have been able to help, and say what sort of help each one could have provided.

   e Work together in groups of three or four. Classify the people and organisations you have listed for **d** into three to six categories by grouping them together. For example, you might group the police, fire and ambulance services together.

   f Agree on a 'heading' for each category, for example 'Emergency Services'. Design a way to record your group's classified ideas clearly.

2. a Read the story of Fiona and Mark Dodd and the 1998 floods.

   b Draw a table with three columns with the headings *before*, *during* and *after*. Write in what the Dodds did and felt during and after the flood. Write in the names of the people and organisations that could have provided help before, during and after the flood.

3. Imagine that you are the Mayor of Northampton. You have been asked to write the Council's Flood Plan. The aim of the plan is to stop or reduce flood problems in the future. It must include three sections:

   ⑤ stopping floods or flood damage from happening

   ⑤ warning people when a flood may happen

   ⑤ responding to the emergency when a flood has happened.

   Use your information about organisations and people who can help *before, during* and *after* a flood in your plan.

A Firefighters organising a rescue in flooded Leamington Spa, 1998

Fiona and Mark Dodd and the 1998 floods

In the weeks before Easter 1998 it rained very heavily across England and Wales.

On *Thursday 9 April*, one month's rain had fallen in 24 hours, and heavy rain was forecast for most of Friday and Saturday in the Midlands.

Fiona and Mark Dodd live with their two young children in Far Cotton near Northampton, close to the River Nene. Just after *midnight*, early on *Friday 10 April*, a policeman called to say that the Environment Agency had put out a flood warning. Half an hour later polluted water swept through the houses in their village. Within minutes the water was 30 cm deep so Mark took the children upstairs. Fiona tried to keep the rising water out with a bucket and pans ... but it was hopeless. They rang Mark's brother, who lives 3 miles away, but he couldn't drive beyond the end of his flooded street.

At *2.00 a.m.* the flood water cut off the power supply. The Dodds tried to move their most valuable possessions upstairs in the dark but in the panic their wedding photographs and earliest pictures of their children were lost. 'How can I tell my daughter as she grows up that I have no photographs of her as a baby?' Fiona cried to a BBC news reporter the following day. 'Our furniture, carpets, washing-machine, television ... everything downstairs is ruined. Our sense of security has been shattered in a terrifying seven hours of cold, wet, pitch-blackness.' Mrs Scott, an elderly neighbour, was filmed as she was carried out of her house by paramedics. She was suffering from hypothermia.

Northamptonshire County Council arranged for flood victims to move into the primary school hall in the next village for the *Easter weekend*. Social Services provided the Dodds and other families with blankets and hot meals.

On *Monday* the Anglian Water Authority pumped the water from the Dodds' street. It smelled awful because of the sewage in it. On *Tuesday* the electrician isolated the sockets downstairs so that the electricity upstairs could be turned on. The assessor from the insurance

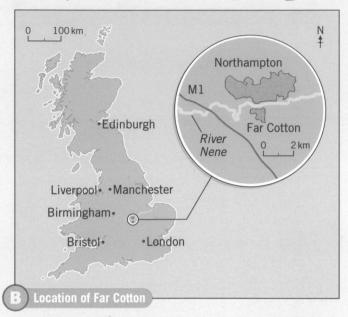

B **Location of Far Cotton**

company came on the *Thursday* and agreed that they needed new carpets.

Over the *next three weeks* Fiona and Mark had to strip the floors down to bare concrete and take the plaster off the walls. Fiona found the constant noise of four dehumidifiers and air-movers very stressful. Their daily struggles with their insurance company and bank put them both under a huge strain.

Mark was critical about the lack of help from the local council: 'Since the flood, we have had no information on health and hygiene precautions or possible pollution effects, except for one leaflet telling us to wash our hands and wear rubber gloves!' He was also angry to discover that the Environment Agency, in charge of flood defences and warnings, had provided sandbags and boats to other flooded areas.

Three months after the flood Fiona and Mark were still shocked and angry: shocked that their lives could have been devastated by flood water sweeping away their possessions; angry that this could have happened without warning. All they could ask was: 'Why did this happen to us?' and 'Could it happen again?'

• ***Based on information from the Environment Agency's Easter 1998 Flood report***

What caused the flooding in Mozambique?

AFRICA

A Mozambique fact file

Area: 801 590 square km (UK 244 100 square km)

Capital: Maputo

Population: 18 million (UK 56 million)

Language: Portuguese, but most people speak local languages, e.g. Swahili

Life expectancy: 47 years

Landscape: Mainly lowland with many large rivers

B

In February 2000 rainfall was much higher than usual for the rainy season. A total of 1163 mm of rain fell during the month compared with the average of 177 mm. The area around Maputo received 455 mm of rain in only 3 days. It led to the worst flooding in southern Mozambique for 40 years. Heavy rains also caused problems in Zimbabwe. Eight-metre-high waves rushed down the Limpopo and Incomati rivers and into Mozambique. As there was no warning system between the two countries the people of Mozambique could do nothing to prepare themselves.

C

By **February 20** the government announced that over 300 000 people had lost their homes. Then on **February 21** cyclone Eline hit southern Mozambique. It destroyed roads, ripped roofs off houses, cut electricity and telephone lines and increased the rainfall. In Zambia huge floods were caused when the overspill gates of the giant Kariba Dam were opened to stop them from bursting. Southern areas of Mozambique were worst affected with over 100 000 hectares of farm land flooded. People have since claimed that some farming and building methods may have made the floods worse.

Activities

1 Create a fact file for Mozambique using an atlas. Use the information in **A** as a starting point. Include information such as *average temperature*, *average rainfall*, *vegetation*, *wealth*, *land use*, *crops* and *population density*.

2 a The flooding between the cities of Maputo and Xai-Xai was at least 5 metres deep. Measure the distance in kilometres between these two cities.

b If this flooding had happened where you live, how far would it stretch? Name a place that is the same distance from your home as Maputo is from Xai-Xai.

3 Draw a table with two columns like the one below. Write in the *physical* and *human* causes of this flooding disaster.

Physical causes	Human causes

The effects of the floods in Mozambique

For two weeks, Joao Nhassengo had no idea whether his family was alive. He first heard of the floods in his own country of Mozambique on the radio at the Johannesburg gold mines where he works. With a one-week pass from work in hand, he rushed home, where he discovered his village underwater and his family gone.

When the water had dropped to waist deep he made his way back to his home, but there was still no word of his family. Then two days ago his wife, Beatriz, returned. 'When I saw her coming across the field on her own, I thought the children must be dead or very sick.' To his joy, he learned that the children had survived and were in a camp.

Now they are all together again. The children have stomach pains caused by drinking the polluted floodwater.

Many of their neighbours have caught cholera from it. Their home is wrecked. The force of the water smashed all the windows and ripped the doors from their hinges. It tore away part of the roof.

But most important are the crops. Beatriz, who is 21, worked a patch of ground nearly five metres wide by 12 metres long. This land fed her family, and, if there was a good harvest, supplied a little extra cash. 'The hoes are still in the house. That is a start, but the maize is ruined.'

'It is something to survive. My children are alive. My house I can rebuild. My crops will grow again. There are many struggles in life. This is just one.'

Adapted from *The Guardian*, Friday 10 March, 2000

The TV cameras have gone but the misery goes on in Mozambique. The water wrecked or damaged the homes of about 250 000 people. Most factories were largely untouched by the floods. However, there was considerable damage to the roads and railways used for trade.

The government estimates that it will need £175 million to rebuild the 620 miles of roads and long stretches of railway track that were swept away. Then there are the electricity and telephone lines and more than 600 schools in need of repair.

Adapted from *The Guardian*, Tuesday 28 March, 2000

A People abandon their homes taking only what they can carry

B Hundreds of people are cut off from the city of Xai-Xai

TREE PEOPLE FACE WILDLIFE PERIL

Celeste Limbombo said her clothes and head were covered in bugs for days. 'Sometimes I couldn't open my eyes because the insects crawled into them. There was no food and drinking the water made me sick. If you are in a tree you have to do all your private things in front of everybody. If you are young it is easy; you can climb down to the water. If you are old it is very hard to move.'

The Guardian, Saturday 4 March, 2000

C Rescue arrives just in time for these flood victims, but they are the lucky ones

D A flooded village near to the Limpopo River

Forty-one helicopters and 15 planes flying from Maputo and Beira are transporting food and medical supplies. So far 14 000 people have been airlifted to safety by six South African helicopters. But there are too few to pluck all the survivors from the flood and many have lived in trees for days.

One helicopter pilot wept as he described his desperation at being able to save just a few dozen people at a time. 'People are just disappearing. We can't get to them all in time. We see people waving from the roofs of houses and when we fly back they're gone' he said.

One woman threw her baby at a full helicopter as it lifted off. A crew member caught the child but the mother's fate is unknown.

Daily Telegraph, **Tuesday 29 March, 2000**

- ✪ The United Nations has appealed for £9.1 million in emergency aid for Mozambique.
- ✪ Britain has donated £5.8 million and cancelled Mozambique's debts.
- ✪ British aid included 100 boats and life rafts, 30 emergency rescue workers, a military team, four RAF helicopters and money to hire further helicopters.
- ✪ The charities Action Aid, Save the Children, Oxfam, Cafod, Christian Aid, Red Cross, Concern, Help the Aged, Merlin, Tear Fund and World Vision have all helped.
- ✪ Italy provided £3.3 million in aid and Japan gave £62,500 in tents and equipment.
- ✪ The French relief agency Médecins du Monde sent a five-person team and 10 tonnes of medical equipment.

Activities

1. Draw a very large **Venn diagram** like the one opposite. On the diagram write in:
   - ◎ the effects of flooding in the *United Kingdom*, in *Mozambique* and in *both countries* in one colour
   - ◎ people's responses to the flooding in the *United Kingdom*, in *Mozambique* and in *both countries* in a second colour.

   Draw a key for the two colours.

2. Use the information in your Venn diagram to write a comparison of the flooding in the United Kingdom and in Mozambique. You should include two side-headings:
   The effects of flooding in the United Kingdom and in Mozambique and
   People's responses to the flooding in the United Kingdom and in Mozambique.
   Under each heading you should mention the *similarities* and *differences* between the two places.

How to ...

... draw a Venn diagram

1. Draw two interlocking circles, large enough to write in, as shown below.

2. Label each circle. In this case, use United Kingdom and Mozambique.

3. Write the names of any shared effects and responses in the overlapping sections.

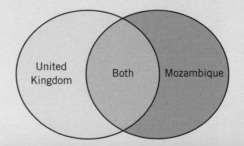

United Kingdom — Both — Mozambique

Review and reflect

Flood disaster – how do people cope?

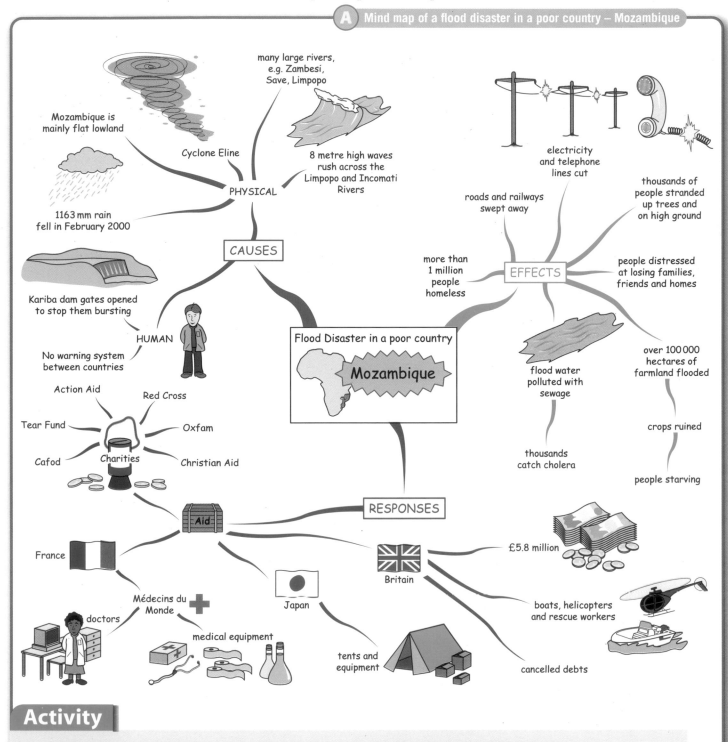

Activity

Look carefully at the mind map above. It shows information about the flood disaster in Mozambique – a poor country. Use it as a model to draw a similar mind map for the United Kingdom – a rich country.

Use information from pages 78–83 of this book as a starting point. If you are able to, add facts from research you have done.

Exploring England

A

B

C

D

Learn about

People have different *perceptions* about places. You are going to look at the images and viewpoints you have of England, and find out if they are correct. In this chapter you are going to learn about:

- what England is really like
- what you mean by England
- what images you have of England
- locating places in England
- England's weather.

What is England really like?

Jasbir, aged 11 A

66 It's not fair that so many people in London are wealthy. 99

Kerrie, aged 14 B

66 England is a great place, because it's full of old buildings, narrow streets, cathedrals and many attractions. 99

Heidi, aged 12 C

66 English food is boring – all those fish and chips! 99

Asma, aged 13 D

66 England is a leading world power. 99

Carl, aged 15 E

66 Stratford-upon-Avon is the birthplace of William Shakespeare. 99

Amy, aged 14 F

66 England is a multi-cultural society. 99

Joe, aged 17 G

66 England has a famous monarchy. 99

...ett, aged 11 H

The River Severn is England's ...gest natural waterway. 99

Su-yin, aged 16 I

66 English weather is OK – when the rain stops! 99

Activities

1. Study quotes **A** to **I** about England and decide which are facts and which are opinions. Organise them into a copy of the table below.

Facts	Opinions

2. Choose one fact and one opinion from your list.

   a How did you decide that something was a fact?

   b How did you decide that something was an opinion?

3. Investigate people's viewpoints in your own class or family.

   a How do they compare with the views of people shown here?

   b Why do you think people have different **perceptions** of England?

What do you mean by England?

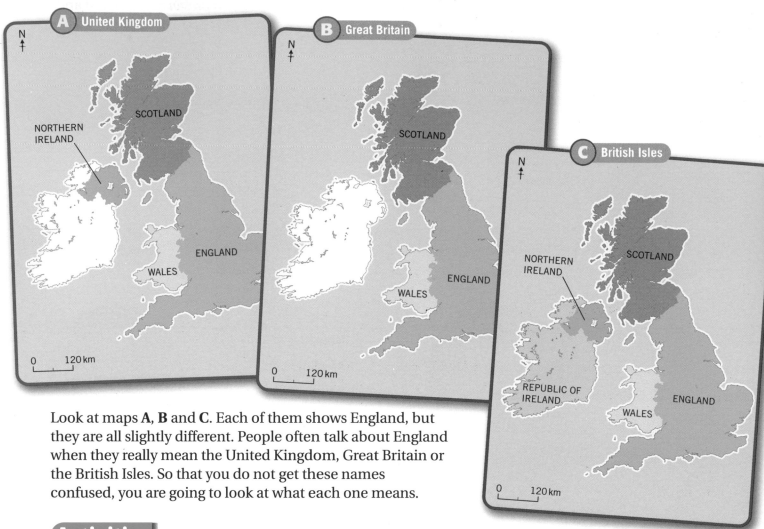

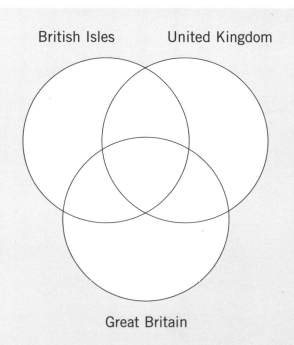

Look at maps **A**, **B** and **C**. Each of them shows England, but they are all slightly different. People often talk about England when they really mean the United Kingdom, Great Britain or the British Isles. So that you do not get these names confused, you are going to look at what each one means.

Activities

1. Draw a Venn diagram, like the one opposite, to show the United Kingdom, Great Britain and the British Isles.

2. In a group, discuss why you think England is part of all three maps **A**, **B** and **C**.

3. Use your Venn diagram and the ideas from your discussion to write a paragraph about England.

4. Complete the sets in the table to show minor places that are part of each whole place. Use an atlas showing the British Isles to help you.

England	Wales	Scotland	Northern Ireland	Republic of Ireland
Surrey	Cardiff			
London	Anglesey			
East Anglia				

British Isles   United Kingdom

Great Britain

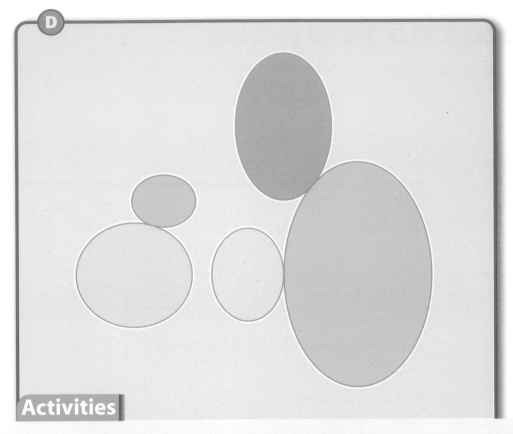

Figure **D** shows a different way of *representing* England and the countries around it. It is a good idea to illustrate something in a different way because it makes you think about what it really shows.

Activities

1 Look at **D**. Find another way to represent England using your own **symbols**.

2 Using an atlas, label your map of England with:

   a five upland areas   **b** five cities
   c five rivers   **d** the place where you live.

  Check the atlas to make sure you use the correct symbols for each of these.

3 **Extension**
England, the United Kingdom, Great Britain and the British Isles make up parts of Europe and the whole world. Using symbols or a map, show how:
a England is part of Europe   **b** England is part of the world.

  Try to think creatively and be imaginative in how you represent the connections.

	England	Scotland	Wales	Northern Ireland	Republic of Ireland
Population (millions)	48.5	5	3	1.5	3.5
Area (km²)	130 000	77 000	21 000	13 500	69 000

E Population and area statistics for parts of the British Isles

4 Copy out the table below. Complete it by regrouping the information from table **E**. 123

	United Kingdom	Great Britain	British Isles
Population (millions)			
Area (km²)			

5 Write five bulleted statements to summarise the differences in population and area between the United Kingdom, Great Britain and the British Isles.

What images do you have of England?

Activities

1 Look at images **A** to **I**. Decide which of these categories each image belongs to:

⊚ definitely in England   ⊚ unlikely to be in England

⊚ probably in England   ⊚ definitely not in England.

2 Share your ideas with the rest of your group. Be prepared to *justify* your ideas.

3 Choose one of the images that you decided was 'definitely in England'. Answer these questions about your chosen image.

a Why is it England?

d Who would live or visit there?

b Where could it be in England?

e Will the place always be like it is now?

c What impressions does the image give you?

4 Is the image you chose an accurate reflection of what England is like?

Where are you in England?

To identify places, you need to think about their characteristics and features. Every place is unique, from the largest city to the smallest village. The place where you live has its own identity.

Activities

1 Where am I?

This place:

- was known as 'the city of a thousand trades'
- is famous for its balti restaurants
- has more canals than Venice
- is home to the International Convention Centre
- has a Premier League football team based at Villa Park
- is where Cadbury's chocolate originated
- has a well known road network nicknamed 'Spaghetti Junction'
- is England's second city
- is home to people who are often called 'Brummies'.

2 Each member of a group in turn thinks of a place. The rest of the group must try to find out the identity of the place by asking questions. They must guess the place within ten questions. The help box gives you suggestions of how to ask questions.

(ICT) Research activity

3 Investigate the images Birmingham presents of itself on the Internet: www.birmingham.gov.uk.

help!

There are many different ways of finding out information. To find out more about a place, you could start your questions with the words:

- What ...?
- Where ...?
- When ...?
- Why ...?
- Who ...?

See also page 10.

What is the weather like?

Weather in the British Isles is always changing – it can be rainy, windy, sunny, cold and warm, sometimes all in the same day. These different types of weather make up Britain's mild and moist climate, which is said to be **temperate**.

Activities

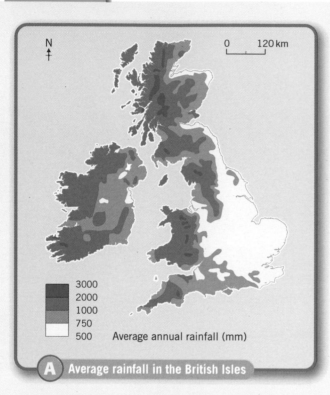

3000
2000
1000
750
500   Average annual rainfall (mm)

A Average rainfall in the British Isles

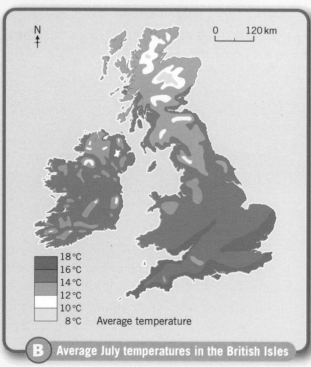

18 °C
16 °C
14 °C
12 °C
10 °C
8 °C   Average temperature

B Average July temperatures in the British Isles

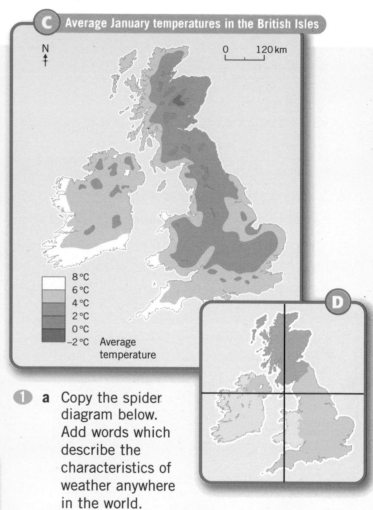

8 °C
6 °C
4 °C
2 °C
0 °C
−2 °C   Average
temperature

C Average January temperatures in the British Isles

D

① **a** Copy the spider diagram below. Add words which describe the characteristics of weather anywhere in the world.

b Underline or colour-code words which are only true of weather in the British Isles. Discuss your choice with a partner – how did you make the selection?

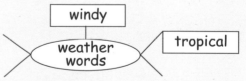

windy

weather
words

tropical

② **a** In pairs, divide a blank map of the British Isles into four areas, like the one in **D**.

b For one area, investigate the weather characteristics by using maps **A** to **C**. Work out a way to show the characteristics on your own map.

c With other pairs, make a full map of the British Isles. Share your information about each area.

Location	Average annual rainfall (mm)	Height of land above sea level (m)
Scafell Pike	2500	978
The Fens (East Anglia)	600	0
South Downs	750	255
Chiltern Hills	650	240
Pennines	1200	693
Cheviot Hills	1000	816
Dartmoor	1500	621

E Rainfall and height above sea level for some English locations

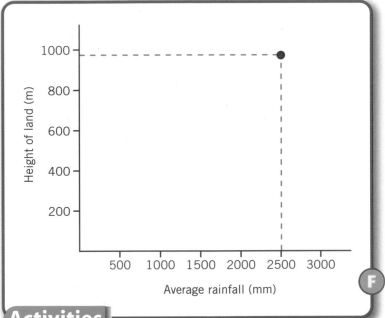

F

How to...

... draw a scattergraph

1 Label the vertical (*y*) axis with the height of the land (m).

2 Label the horizontal (*x*) axis with the average rainfall (mm).

3 For Scafell Pike:
   - go up the *y* axis to 978 m.
   - go along the *x* axis to 2500 mm.
   - plot a point where the two lines meet.

4 Repeat for all the other places on the table.

Activities

3 Use the help box on page 98 to write an account of England's weather in winter and summer.

4 Study the figures on table **E**. Plot the values for each place onto a scattergraph of rainfall and height like the one if **F**. The How to ... box shows you what to do. **123**

5 Look carefully at your graph. Can you see a relationship between rainfall and the height of the land? **123**

6 Use your graph to write a summary explaining the relationship between rainfall and the height of the land.

7 **a** Make a copy of the location and weather grid opposite. Use all the information on these pages and an atlas to fill in the remaining spaces on the grid.

b Can you see any relationships within the grid, for example between relief and other features?

Relief:	Mountainous	Hilly	Flat
Rainfall			
Population			
Other features, e.g roads			

Getting Technical ▼

You will find more information about weather in England at www.meto.gov.uk

Why does Britain's weather change?

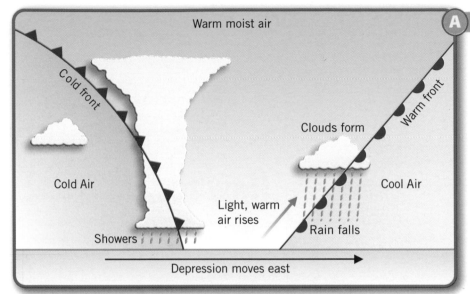

A A cross-section through a depression

Warm moist air

Cold front

Warm front

Cold Air

Clouds form

Cool Air

Light, warm
air rises

Rain falls

Showers

Depression moves east

Britain's weather is influenced by two types of **weather systems**:

- **anticyclones** (high pressure) bring settled weather – hot in summer, cold in winter

- **depressions** (low pressure) bring changeable weather – often rain, cloud and wind.

B Weather chart for north-west Europe, 12 June 2000

00

84

76

L
970

08

16

H
1032

H
1031

L
1020

Depressions form over the Atlantic Ocean and move from west to east towards the British Isles. The low pressure draws in warm, moist air from the south, and cold air from the north. The warm and cold air masses do not mix. Where they meet, the boundary between them is called a **front**.

Most depressions take one to three days to cross the British Isles, and they bring with them one or more fronts. Figure **A** shows what happens to the weather near a front:

- warm air is lighter, so it is forced over the cold air mass

- as the warm air rises, it cools down. Moisture condenses into clouds which often bring rain

- air is sucked into the low-pressure system, causing winds which blow in an anti-clockwise direction.

Map **B** is a **synoptic chart** for north-west Europe on 12 June 2000. It shows a depression south of Iceland (970 mb) and an anticyclone south-west of the British Isles (1032 mb).

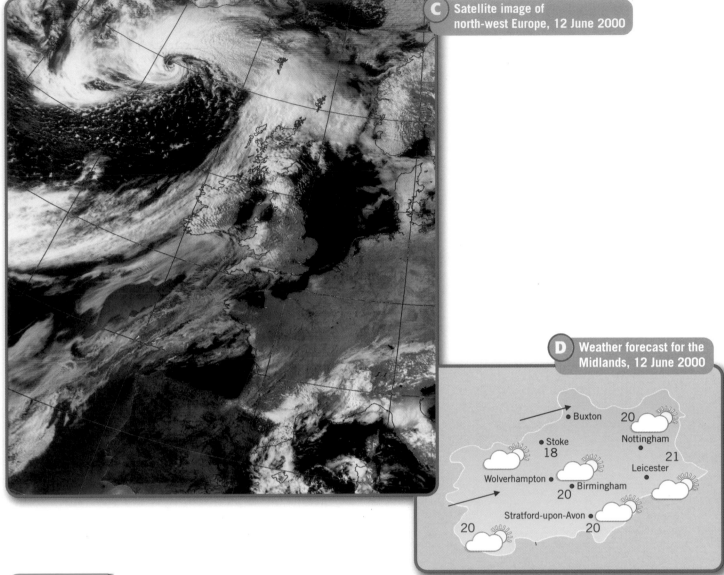

C Satellite image of north-west Europe, 12 June 2000

D Weather forecast for the Midlands, 12 June 2000

- Buxton 20
- Stoke 18 Nottingham
  Leicester 21
Wolverhampton • • Birmingham
20
Stratford-upon-Avon •
20 20

Activities

1 Read the text and make a list of the characteristics of a depression. Use these headings to help:
- pressure
- wind
- rainfall.

2 a Study map **B**. Make a tracing of the fronts, the area of low pressure and high pressure around the British Isles. Then put your tracing over the satellite image **C** and shade on the area of cloud.

b Add labels to your tracing to help describe and explain the weather over the British Isles. Use your list from question **1** to help you.

3 In groups of five or six, plan a mime of the processes involved in the formation and development of a depression. Use the key words from the text and your answers to activities **1–3** to help you. Show your mime to the rest of the class, then use key words to explain what is happening.

4 **Extension**
Study weather map **D** for the West Midlands.
a Describe the weather on Monday 12 June.
b Use satellite image **C** and synoptic chart **B** to forecast what you think will happen to the weather on Tuesday 13 June.
c Draw a simple weather map for the weather forecast on Tuesday 13 June.

Planning a tour of England

A

MEMORANDUM

FROM: *Area Manager*

TO: *Tour operator*

A party of 55 visitors from the United States will be arriving at Heathrow Airport, London on Monday at 7.00 am to stay for five days.

They want to see at least seven typically English attractions. Please design their trip and get back to me as soon as possible.

Please note that the group can only travel 300 km (180 miles) per day, so timings are very important.

You will also need to think about the weather people might encounter in different parts of England in June. Think carefully about departure times and the routes used – make these clear on your plan.

Good luck!

B

Activities

1 Read the memo from Sunshine Tours. In pairs, plan a journey to fulfil all their requirements.

help!

When you do any activity, you naturally follow through a **process of thinking**. This is outlined below. Work through each stage in turn to achieve a structured and accurate piece of work.

- ✪ **Cueing** Think about what you want to include in your tour.

- ✪ **Acting** Decide on what you are going to do, then design the first draft of your tour.

- ✪ **Monitoring** Is your tour meeting all the requirements? Should you add anything or take something out? Design your final piece of work.

- ✪ **Verifying** Is your tour complete? Check with your teacher. Share your tour ideas with others.

2 On a map of England, show the destinations, features, routes travelled, distances and timings. Use a different colour for each destination.

3 **Extension**
Use a desktop publishing package to publish an advertising poster or leaflet about your tour. ICT

4 **Research activity**
Explore England on the Internet at www.travelengland.org.uk. Choose one region or place you think visitors from the USA might visit on their tour. ICT

5 Create a word bank of the words you have learned in this unit about England. 📖

Review and reflect

Odd one out

1 Perceptions	14 Northern Ireland	27 Facts
2 England	15 Republic of Ireland	28 Opinions
3 Images	16 Categories	29 Cueing
4 Weather	17 Reflection	30 Acting
5 United Kingdom	18 Accurate	31 Monitoring
6 Great Britain	19 Justify	32 Verifying
7 British Isles	20 Location	33 Destinations
8 Describe	21 Features	34 Advertise
9 Represent	22 Characteristic	35 Temperate
10 Illustrate	23 Identify	36 Climate
11 Symbol	24 Explore	37 Predict
12 Scotland	25 Promote	38 Actual
13 Wales	26 Places	

Activities

1 In pairs, look at each set of numbers below. For each set:

  a Find the four words in the list that match the numbers.

  b Try to decide which word is the odd one out.

  c Explain why it is the odd one out and what the other three have in common.

Set A	4	6	35	36
Set B	1	17	27	28
Set C	2	5	12	13
Set D	3	20	24	26
Set E	10	11	16	21

2 Next, design some other sets to try out on your partner.

3 Organise all the words on the list into groups. You may have from three to six groups, each with a descriptive heading or title.

4 Reflect

Look back at the images of England that have been used in this chapter, or in the whole book. Discuss with a partner:

  ⑤ which places have been included   ⑤ which people have been included

  ⑤ which have been left out   ⑤ which have been left out.

Write a short letter to the authors presenting your findings and your point of view.

6 World sport

Learn about

Sport is enjoyed by people all over the world. In this unit you will learn:

- how people take part in or watch sport
- where football grounds are located, and the reasons for this
- how football grounds have an impact on people and environments
- why the football industry is changing, and the effects this may have
- how to investigate patterns or changes in sport.

A Sport is important to large international companies ...

C People like to watch sport ...

B ... and to small local businesses

D ... and to take part themselves

Soundbites on sport

Sport is an athletic activity, a game or a pastime. Some sports, such as fishing, are done by individual people. Other sports, such as football or netball, are team events. People take part in sport to have fun, to keep fit, to make friends, to compete against others, or to relax.

Sport is becoming more important every year because, as countries develop, many people have more free time and more money to spend. One way to enjoy free time and spend money is to play or watch a sport.

Sport is big business worldwide and involves companies of all sizes. **Multinational** corporations such as Nike, BSkyB and Coca-Cola invest hundreds of millions of pounds in sport every year (see **A**), while small local shops sell fishing tackle and tyre-repair kits (**B**).

Sport brings pleasure to people who watch it (see table **E**). Adults and children both also enjoy actively taking part in sport, although there are some differences in the sports they prefer (table **F**). However, people's lives in the UK are changing. Between 1990 and 2000, fewer people went to watch big sporting events, and fewer actively took part in sport.

Sport	Percentage of adults
Football	12.2
Cricket	3.7
Horse racing	3.4
Rugby Union	3.4
Motor racing	3.1

E The top five sports that adults paid to watch (1998)

Aged 11–14		Adults	
Cycling	48	Walking	22
Swimming	41	Aerobics, keep fit, gym	20
Football	33	Swimming	18
Tennis	25	Cycling	9
Walking	18	Golf	8

Figures are percentages that take part in the sport. Some people do more than one sport.

F Taking part: the top five sports in the UK (1998)

Activities

1. a Choose the type of graph that would best show the data in table **E**.

   b Draw the graph and describe what it shows.

   c Choose a different style of graph that would best show the data in table **F**.

   d Draw the graph and describe what it shows. (1 2 3)

2. Study the photos on the opposite page. Discuss with a partner the way in which sport and money are linked. Make a list of as many ways as you can think of.

3. Investigate the sporting activities of the people in your class, both in and out of school. These questions may help you.

   ⊚ Are young people's sporting activities different from those of adults (see **F**)?

   ⊚ Are activities different for girls and boys?

   ⊚ Do activities vary according to where people live?

help!

Remember the four steps in an enquiry (see pages 10–17):

○ first ask questions

○ then collect information

○ show your results

○ finally make your conclusions.

Football – the world's favourite sport

Football is certainly the biggest sport in the world in business terms. The 'world game' is the most popular sport on Earth, and even countries such as the USA and China, not traditionally footballing nations, are big fans. FIFA, football's international governing body, estimates that football generates £123 billion of economic activity each year, and the month-long World Cup finals draw the largest audience of any televised event in the world.

Football was first played in Britain in the 1870s, and England's Premiership League is among the most famous in the world. The Premiership League includes teams from England and sometimes Wales. Scotland has its own league, as do Northern Ireland and the Republic of Ireland.

Arsenal (North London)	Leicester City
Aston Villa (Birmingham)	Liverpool
Bradford	Manchester City
Charlton Athletic (London)	Manchester United
Chelsea (West London)	Middlesbrough
Coventry City	Newcastle United
Derby County	Southampton
Everton (Liverpool)	Sunderland
Ipswich Town	Tottenham Hotspur (North London)
Leeds United	West Ham United (East London)

A The teams in the Premiership League for 2000–2001

Manchester United is one of the most famous and certainly the most successful of all football teams. You can find their website at http://www.manutd.com. Their players come from a number of countries (see table **B**). This is partly because they are among the world's best players but also because it helps sell Manchester United and Manchester United's products if there are players from many countries. For example, if Manchester United were to buy a famous Brazilian footballer, sales of their goods in South America would go up.

Manchester United won the European Champions Cup in 1999 for the first time since 1968. Their route to the final is shown in **C**.

Player	Country of origin
Mark Bosnich	Australia
Gary Neville	England
Jaap Stam	Holland (Netherlands)
Michel Silvestre	France
Phil Neville	England
Paul Scholes	England
Dwight Yorke	Trinidad and Tobago
Roy Keane	Ireland
Denis Irwin	Ireland
Ryan Giggs	Wales
Nicky Butt	England
Quintan Fortune	South Africa
Teddy Sheringham	England
Andy Cole	England
Ole Gunnar Solskjaer	Norway
David Beckham	England
Jordi Cruyff	Holland (Netherlands)
Ronny Johnsen	Norway
Raymond van de Gouw	Holland (Netherlands)
Wes Brown	England
Ronnie Wallwork	England
Jonathan Greening	England
Alex Ferguson (Manager)	Scotland

B The countries of origin of Manchester United players, 1999–2000

C Manchester United's European Cup campaign, 1998–1999

Preliminary round

Łódż (Poland)

Group round

Brondby (Denmark)
Bayern Munich (Germany)
Barcelona (Spain)

Quarter Final

Inter Milan (Italy)

Semi Final

Juventus (Turin, Italy)

Final

Bayern Munich (Germany): match played in Barcelona

D The Manchester United team, before playing against Real Madrid in the Opel Masters 2000 Tournament in Munich

Activities

1 On an outline map of England and Wales, plot the *distribution* of football teams in the 2000–2001 Premiership League.

2 Find a list of Premiership clubs from an earlier year. Plot the distribution for that year in a different colour.

3 Describe the distributions you have drawn. Refer to clusters of teams as well as to areas where there are few teams. Is there any pattern to the distribution? Are there more teams in the north of England than in the south? Do most teams come from large cities?

4 On an outline map of the world, show the countries of origin of players who played for Manchester United in 1999–2000. Comment on the distribution you have plotted.

5 In every round of the European Cup except the Final, teams play one match at home and one away against each opposing team.

  a On an outline map of Europe, show where Manchester United played their away matches in 1998–1999.

b In how many countries did they play?

c Which was the furthest match from their home in Manchester?

d Which was the nearest?

ICT Research activity

6 Bring your work up to date by doing some research. Use team websites or newspapers to help you. Choose a league team you support or that plays near your home.

  a Find out the countries of origin of the players in your team. Compare them with those for Manchester United in question **4**.

  b Draw a map to show how your team, or your national team, played their way through another international competition. Follow the steps in question **5**.

Getting to a football match

Following a football team and travelling to their away matches can be quite expensive, and it certainly needs some careful planning. You may have to travel from one end of the country to another to follow your favourite team. You would need to decide which type of transport best suits your journey, remembering that some forms of transport are cheaper than others.

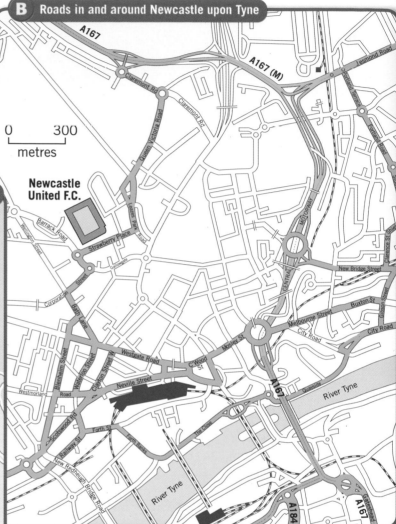

B Roads in and around Newcastle upon Tyne

Newcastle United F.C.

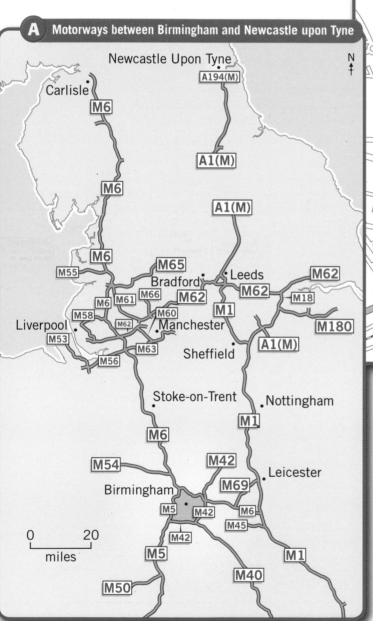

A Motorways between Birmingham and Newcastle upon Tyne

The Third Round of the Cup

Imagine that you live in Birmingham and your team has been drawn to play away against Newcastle United in the FA Cup. You live on the north side of Birmingham close to the M6, and your family decides to drive to Newcastle upon Tyne using the motorway network shown in map **A**.

Activities

1. Describe the route you would take from Birmingham to Newcastle to watch the football match. Look carefully at **B**, which shows roads in and around Newcastle. To get into Newcastle you follow the A184 from the A194 (M).

The Fourth Round of the Cup

After beating Newcastle United your team now has to play away against Chelsea. This time your family decides to take the train. You have to travel by train from Birmingham New Street to London (see **C**) and then take a London Underground train to Fulham Broadway, the nearest station to Chelsea's ground at Stamford Bridge (see **D**).

D London Underground map

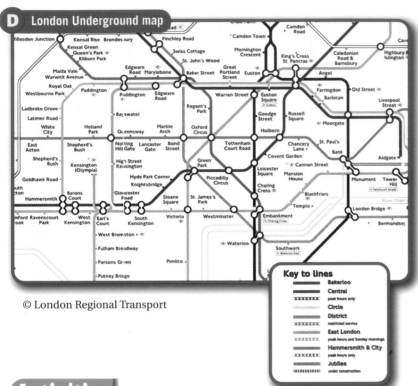

© London Regional Transport

Key to lines

▬▬▬	Bakerloo
▬▬▬	Central
▪▪▪▪	peak hours only
▪▪▪▪	Circle
▬▬▬	District
▪▪▪▪	restricted service
▬▬▬	East London
▬▬▬	peak hours and Sunday mornings
▬▬▬	Hammersmith & City
▪▪▪▪	peak hours only
▬▬▬	Jubilee
▪▪▪▪	under construction

C Trains from Birmingham to London

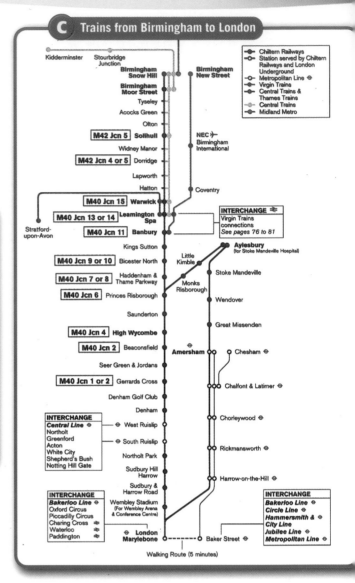

Walking Route (5 minutes)

Activities

2 a Use **C** to decide which railway line you should use, and which London station you will get off at.

b Decide which Underground trains you will use to get to Fulham Broadway (see map **D**).

c Write out a detailed journey planner to show clearly how to get from Birmingham New Street to Fulham Broadway.

3 The distance from Birmingham to Newcastle is approximately 320 km. The train takes three hours and costs £60 return. London is approximately 190 km away from Birmingham. The train from Birmingham to London takes 1 hour 50 minutes (fast) or 2 hours 30 minutes (slow) and costs £23.50 (fast) or £13.90 (slow) return.

a Which is the most cost-effective route in terms of price per kilometre travelled?

b Which is the best route in terms of journey time per kilometre? **①②③**

4 a If a car travels at an average speed of 80 km/hour, how long will it take to travel from Birmingham to:

   i Newcastle?   **ii** London?

b The petrol needed to travel 1 km costs about 8p. How much would the petrol cost for each journey?

c What other costs are involved in running a car? **①②③**

5 In a group, discuss which would be the best way to make each of the journeys for:

a someone travelling alone   **b** a family of four.

Think about journey time and cost. You might also think about factors such as convenience and pollution. **①②③**

Football – a changing industry

Football attendances

In 1949–1950 attendance at football league matches in Britain peaked at over 40 million people. By 1985–1986 this had fallen by over 60 per cent to just over 16 million. This fall has been blamed on competing forms of recreation and leisure, and also on hooliganism at football matches. Since 1985–1986 attendances have increased, due to safety measures taken at grounds, a fall in hooliganism and media attention.

Football crowds are also changing. In the past, fans came from working-class backgrounds, and this is still often the case for clubs in the lower divisions. However, due to increases in entrance fees and improvements in facilities, many of the Premiership clubs attract an increasing number of wealthier supporters. Some people say that this is because only wealthy people can afford tickets to watch the large clubs play.

Funding

Many football clubs operate at a loss because they have to pay very large salaries and transfer fees and maintain their grounds, facilities and equipment. Clubs receive income from a number of sources.

 Sponsorship – clubs earn money through shirt sponsorship. This gives the sponsor much publicity, which is great if the club is doing well. Match programmes can also be sponsored. Money can be made from corporate hospitality, where companies pay to use the club's facilities to entertain would-be customers.

 Advertising – clubs sell advertising space on boards that surround the pitch and in the match programme.

 Ticket sales – the money taken at the gates for league matches is kept by the home team. Small clubs only take a small amount of money. In the FA Cup and Coca-Cola Cup, the ticket money is shared between the teams, so a small club that plays a big club may earn a large sum of money.

 Television fees – about £25 million is available to clubs in the Nationwide League from the TV companies.

- 75 per cent goes to Division One clubs
- 18 per cent goes to Division Two clubs
- 7 per cent goes to Division Three clubs.

BSkyB paid the Premiership League a huge £670 million to televise matches live in the 2000–2001 season.

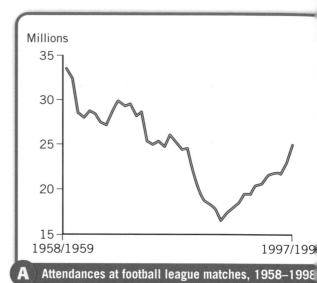

A Attendances at football league matches, 1958–1998

B Arrests and attendances at football league matches, 1984–1995

C Football is played all over the world and is sponsored by world famous companies

- Merchandising – most clubs have a shop which sells football kits, scarves and other merchandise.
- Sale of players – clubs also sell players to make money. Clubs in Divisions Two and Three may have to sell their better players to bigger clubs in order to raise funds to pay the wages of the club's other players and staff.

Recent changes in the football industry

There have been many developments in recent years:

- increased safety requirements
- the creation of the Premier League in 1992–1993
- increased media coverage from BSkyB
- the development of football as an industry, with some clubs now companies on the Stock Exchange
- huge increases in players' salaries and transfer fees
- redevelopment and relocation of football grounds.

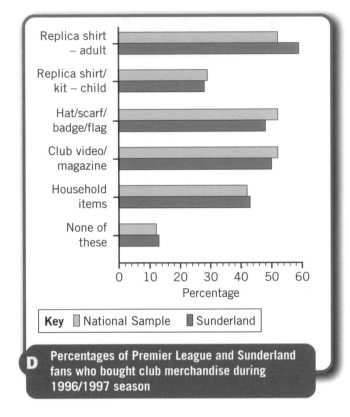

Key ■ National Sample ■ Sunderland

D Percentages of Premier League and Sunderland fans who bought club merchandise during 1996/1997 season

Activities

1. Study photograph **C**. How many different sorts of sponsorship can you see? Make a short list of ways in which sponsorship helps the club and the sponsor.

2. a Graph **A** is a *line graph*. Discuss with a partner what it tells you about football attendances.
   b Use the help box to help you write a short summary of your findings. (123)

3. a Study graph **B**. With a partner, discuss what it tells you about attendances at football matches, compared with arrests for hooliganism.
   b Use the help box again to write a short summary of your findings. (123)

4. Graph **D** is a *bar graph*. Because it has two different types of bar, it can also be called a *multiple bar graph*. Use the help box to investigate what the data shows. Make sure you:
   - describe which sorts of merchandise are most popular, and which are least popular.
   - compare the information about Sunderland fans with that about fans across England and Wales. (123)

5. Which graph do you think shows the information best? Which is easiest to use? Give reasons for your answer. (123)

Research activity

6. Investigate the pattern of support for football in your class. You could focus on:
   - which teams students support
   - how often students watch football on TV, or attend matches
   - what merchandising students have, and what they think about it.

   Show your results using the best sorts of graphs for the data you have collected. Then make your conclusions. (123)

help!

Geographers often use graphs to show data. Graphs help them to investigate patterns and changes in the world around us. When you use graphs to investigate, try to:

- start with a sentence saying what the graph is about
- look for general patterns and changes (describe)
- include figures and examples
- if possible, think of some reasons for what you've found out (explain).

Where are football grounds located?

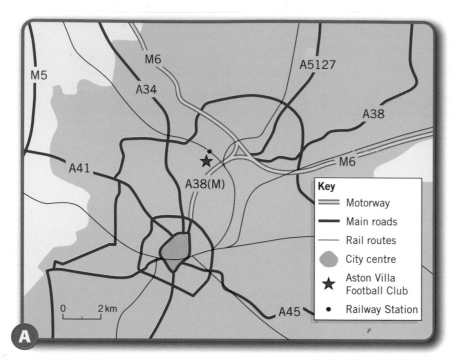

A

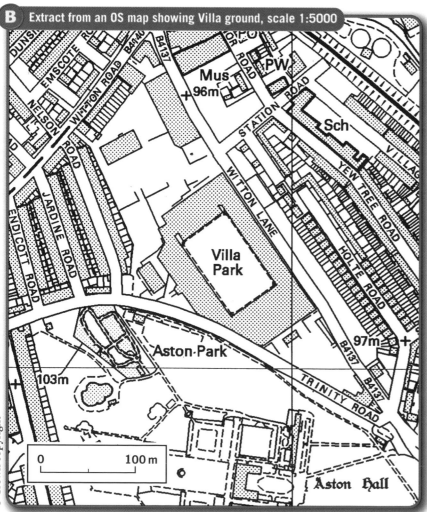

B Extract from an OS map showing Villa ground, scale 1:5000

Change at Aston Villa

Aston Villa Football Club started in 1874 as an amateur church team. The club grew and prospered and in 1897 they won the league and cup double. In the same year they moved to a new ground at Villa Park, **located** on parkland close to the northern edge of Birmingham. Working-class housing and industry quickly surrounded the ground. Today the area is very built up and far from the edge of the city. The club has plans to expand its ground but this has led to conflict with the local community.

The people of Aston

Twenty thousand people live in the area, 49 per cent of them young people under 24. The local community comes from many backgrounds, including 51 per cent Asian, 31 per cent white, and 14 per cent black people. Unemployment in the area is 23 per cent, compared with 10 per cent for Birmingham as a whole.

The place

Aston is typical of an inner city area built in Victorian times. Most of the housing is terraced. People with cars have to park them on the street. The main area of public open space is Aston Park, in the grounds of historic Aston Hall. There are shops along Witton Lane, large areas of industrial land and some car parks.

The impact of Villa Park

About three-quarters of Villa fans live within 45 minutes' travel time of Aston, and most people travel to the ground by car. Football matches at Villa Park cause a number of problems on match days. These include:

- increased traffic congestion
- on-street parking by football fans
- litter, noise and pollution
- antisocial behaviour
- disruption to people's daily routines.

Aston Villa's plans

The Aston Villa ground has a **capacity** of 39 339. In the 1999–2000 season, it was 81 per cent full on average. The directors of the club want to develop the ground so that it can seat 50 000 supporters – big enough to bring European matches to Birmingham. The club can't rebuild the ground without permission, so it has sent a planning application to the city council. The plans include:

- extending the North Stand and Trinity Road Stand
- redeveloping the Holte Hotel Public House into a 140-bed hotel
- closing or moving Trinity Road
- moving the Aston Play centre
- the loss of a playground, land and trees from the Park.

C Aerial photo of Villa Park and its surroundings

Today Aston Villa employs 200 staff, with more on match days. The increased seating capacity, and new retail, hotel and industrial developments would create more job opportunities for local people.

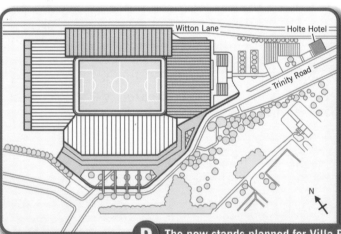

D The new stands planned for Villa Park (shown in yellow)

Activities

1. Study the maps and aerial photo. Draw a sketch map of the area around Villa Park. Add labels to show these land uses: Aston Villa's stadium, terraced housing, industry, Aston Park.

2. Read the text and study the plans for the new stadium.
   a Add to your labels any more details about land use you can find.
   b Mark the planned new stands on your map.

3. Study the list which describes the impact of Villa Park. Choose two or three of the impacts and find evidence from the text, maps or aerial photograph which helps explain them. Then write a short summary about the impact of Villa Park on the local community.

4. Finally, think about the location of Villa Park in 1897 and today. Think about the advantages and disadvantages of its location. You might want to set your work out in a table like this – but you may not need to fill in all the boxes.

	Villa Park in 1897	Villa Park today
Advantages of this location		
Disadvantages of this location		

DOES BIRMINGHAM CITY COUNCIL UNDERSTAND THAT THERE IS NO ROOM FOR VILLA PARK TO EXPAND?

Have the residents of Aston proved their point or not?

On 6 September 1998 more than 2000 people peacefully formed a human chain around the ground to protest against the expansion of the club.

They were protesting that their streets had been taken over by fans and their cars. They had been polluted by car fumes and rubbish had been thrown into their gardens. They had been imprisoned in their homes. Now they were expected to give up Trinity Road, which links the community and their park – the only recreation ground in the area. In return they would be expected to take all the abuse of fans coming into the area and stay quietly locked in their homes.

Aston Villa FC claimed it had been here for over 100 years and certainly before the current residents. This is not fair and the residents of Aston are getting angry. Now they want action to oppose the expansion and also to alleviate the problems being experienced now with the club.

Aston Neighbourhood Forum
Aston Federation of Churches and Mosques

E | **Development compass rose**

Natural:
these are changes to the environment

Who decides:
the people who make decisions about the changes

Economic:
these are changes involving money

Social:
these are changes to people and the way they live

F | **The Villa Ground brings some benefits to the local community**

Activities

1. The development compass rose helps work out the changes brought about by a development.

   a In pairs, make a copy of the compass rose in **E** in the middle of a large piece of paper.

   b Use all the information on pages 108–110 to work out the changes which the plans for Villa Park would bring. Decide whether they are Natural, Economic, or Social, or show Who Decides. Label these onto your compass rose.

   c Colour code your labels to show which you think are changes for the better and which changes for the worse.

2. Discuss with your partner who would *gain* and who would *lose* from the plans to expand the ground. Use a winners and losers grid like the one below to help you:

Winners	Losers
Person: **local shopkeeper**	Person:
Reason:	Reason:
Person:	Person:
Reason:	Reason:
Person:	Person:
Reason:	Reason:

Case Study

Oxford United – a club on the move

In 1995 Oxford United announced that they were to leave their Manor Ground at Headington, because the site was too small. They could not upgrade the stadium with the new safety measures that are now required and were unable to exploit the commercial side of football very effectively. In 1996 the club started to build a new stadium to seat 15 000 people on a larger site with ample parking and room for many more facilities.

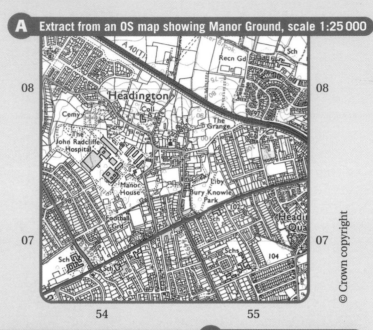

A Extract from an OS map showing Manor Ground, scale 1:25 000

© Crown copyright

The old Manor Ground stadium

The Manor Ground has a 'small club' atmosphere about it. The pitch is small, just 100 m by 68 m (110 yards by 75 yards). The stadium is unsuitable for a modern club, and its capacity has been reduced to under 10 000 fans. It is located in a high

B Manor Ground football ground, Oxford

quality residential area and with poor access, limited parking, few facilities and limited capacity, the club could not survive as a business.

The main entrance to the ground is from the busy A40, the main London Road. This is congested with shoppers most Saturdays during autumn and spring, and with tourist traffic in the summer. The ground is also close to Oxford's main hospital.

Parking congestion during and after matches may make it difficult for ambulances to reach casualties in the local area, or the hospital itself.

However, local residents were not keen to see the club move. A survey showed that, on balance, residents thought that the club brought more advantages than disadvantages. Although some mentioned problems such as congestion on match days, graffiti and noise, over 70 per cent thought that the club brought benefits to the area. These included employment for players, caterers, coaches, groundsmen, physiotherapists and electricians. Football does not just employ footballers!

Because the residential area contains a number of shops and pubs, fans tend to spend money in these rather than in the limited facilities within the ground. This was good for the neighbourhood, but further reduced the business success of Oxford United.

New rules for football stadiums meant that the ground's capacity would have been reduced to just over 5000 fans, not enough to keep the club in business. Because of the limited facilities, the ground was only being used about 25 days each year – not enough to remain profitable.

C Extract from an OS map showing the Minchery Farm site, scale 1:25 000

© Crown copyright

The new stadium at Minchery Farm

With all these considerations in mind, the club decided to develop a new stadium. It would have all the facilities that the club needed, and the site would include a hotel, conference centre, multiplex cinema, banqueting centre, fitness centre, bowling alley, and an all-weather pitch. These would be used throughout the year, not just on match-days. The site will have parking spaces for 2000 cars and 15 coaches.

The new site has a number of advantages over the Headington site.

- There is room for expansion.
- There is room for parking.
- There are no other facilities nearby, so fans will spend more money within the stadium.
- There is plenty of room to develop new facilities.
- It is close to where workers live in the Blackbird Leys and Littlemore areas of Oxford.

D Minchery Farm site, Oxford

Activities

1 Using OS maps **A** and **C** and photos **B** and **D**, copy and complete this site survey for each site. A score of 1 means poor, 7 means excellent. Circle the scores you choose.

Lack of space	1	2	3	4	5	6	7	Plenty of space
No room to expand	1	2	3	4	5	6	7	Room to expand
Limited parking	1	2	3	4	5	6	7	Unlimited parking
Pay to park	1	2	3	4	5	6	7	Free parking
Poor access	1	2	3	4	5	6	7	Good access
Few nearby facilities	1	2	3	4	5	6	7	Many nearby facilities
Expensive land	1	2	3	4	5	6	7	Cheap land
High population density	1	2	3	4	5	6	7	Low population density
Few extra jobs created	1	2	3	4	5	6	7	Many extra jobs created

2 What are the advantages of Oxford United's original site? What are its disadvantages?

3 What are the advantages of the new site at Minchery Farm? What are the disadvantages of that site?

4 Imagine that you are a resident in Headington fed up with the problems caused by people on match days. Write a letter to a local newspaper outlining the problems and suggesting what could be done about them.

5 Imagine that you are a local shopkeeper and that you earn a lot of money from fans on match days. Write a reply to the above letter, arguing in favour of the club, and its impact on the local economy.

6 Choose one football issue: either the plans for Aston Villa (pages 108–110) or for Oxford United (pages 111–112). Write a letter or report for the planning department about the new stand at Aston Villa or the new stadium for Oxford United.

7 **Extension**
Find out if there is a planned relocation or a new sporting development in your home area. Make two lists – one of all the advantages of the new scheme, and one of all the disadvantages. Are you in favour of the development? Use evidence to support your answer.

help!

Good geographers:

- think carefully about their own point of view
- present evidence carefully to support it
- include different types of information, such as sketch maps or labelled photographs
- remember that other people may have different views.

The World Cup

For football fans the FIFA World Cup is the greatest competition in the world. The first World Cup was held in 1930, and it has been held every four years since then, except during World War II. The winners of each football World Cup are shown in **A**.

France won the 1998 World Cup when they beat Brazil 3–0. The quarter-finalist countries are shown in **B**, with the level of economic wealth for each one. Average GDP values for some groups of countries are shown in **C**.

1930	Uruguay	1970	Brazil
1934	Italy	1974	West Germany
1938	Italy	1978	Argentina
1950	Uruguay	1982	Italy
1954	West Germany	1986	Argentina
1958	Brazil	1990	West Germany
1962	Brazil	1994	Brazil
1966	England	1998	France

A World Cup winners

Quarter-finalist	GDP (US $)	Quarter-finalist	GDP (US $)
France	18 554	Germany	21 260
Brazil	2 107	Italy	15 548
Croatia	4 520	Denmark	23 690
Argentina	4 021	Netherlands	18 369

B Quarter-finalists in the 1998 FIFA World Cup

C Average GDP values

	Average GDP (US $)
All developing countries	908
Least developed countries	245
Eastern Europe and the CIS	1 989
Developed countries	19 283
World	3 610

Activities

1. Plot the winners of the World Cup on a map of the world. Use a different colour for those that have won once, twice and three times.

2. Compare your map with world map **D**. Describe the distribution you have drawn, for example by saying how many of the winning countries are developed, European, in the Southern Hemisphere, etc.

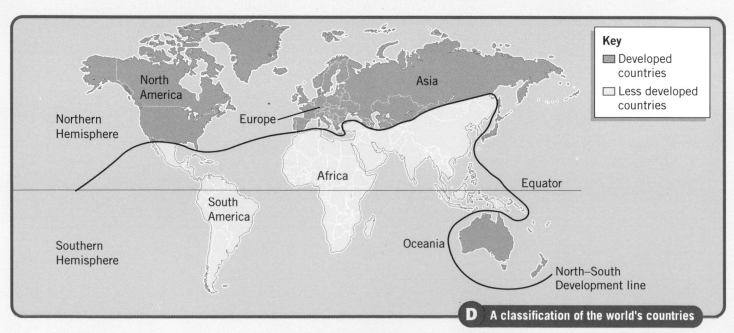

D A classification of the world's countries

3. What evidence is there to suggest that the 1998 quarter-finalists in **B** are drawn mostly from the world's wealthiest countries? Look at **C**, which shows you the average GDP for developed and developing countries. You may want to use an atlas to help you.

Review and reflect

Key enquiry questions	Page numbers	Case studies or examples	What I learned about or did
Who takes part in or watches sport?	101		Planning an enquiry
Where are Premiership clubs located? What are their links with other parts of the world?	102–103		Plot distribution on a map
How do people get to football matches?	104–105		Planning routes
How is the football industry changing?	106–107		Finding information from graphs
Where are football grounds located?	108–113	Aston, Birmingham Oxford	The impact of football grounds on an area
How do people make decisions about changes?	108–113	Aston, Birmingham Oxford	Writing to persuade people
Which are the world's most successful footballing nations?	114		Describing and explaining patterns

Activities

1 Make a large copy of the table above. For each enquiry question, look back at your work for this unit and write the examples or places you have studied in the 'Case studies' column. One has already been done to help you.

2 The fourth column shows at least one thing you should have learned about or done for each enquiry question. For each one, check your work to see where you actually did this. Then add at least one more thing you learned.

3 Write down the three most interesting or important things you have learned about the world of sport. Explain why you chose them.

4 Write down two or three things you did or learned that might be useful in other subject areas.

5 Finally, write down which activities you found most difficult. Choose one or two targets you need to improve on in your next geography unit.

Glossary

Active volcano A volcano that has erupted recently and is likely to erupt again.

Active zone An area where two tectonic plates meet. Earthquakes and volcanoes occur in active zones.

Aid Help that is given by one country to another, either after an emergency such as an earthquake or to help to improve living standards.

Annotated An annotated sketch has labels that describe or explain the features that it shows.

Annual population growth rate The difference between the birth rate and the death rate for a country. It shows whether the population is getting larger or smaller.

Anticyclone A high-pressure weather system that brings settled weather, hot in summer, cold in winter.

Atlas A book of maps that show different physical and human features of the world.

Birth rate The number of babies born to every 1000 people in a country each year.

Capacity The amount or number that something will hold.

Central Business District (CBD) The area of a city where there are many shops and offices.

Climate The average weather conditions of a place or region measured over many years.

Condense Change from a gas into a liquid, for example from water vapour into the water droplets that form clouds.

Confluence The place where two or more streams or rivers join.

Core Very hot rocks in the centre of the Earth.

Crater A wide hole in the ground. The crater of a volcano is the hollow at the top of its opening.

Crust The thin outer layer of the Earth.

Death rate The number of people who die for every 1000 people in a country each year.

Depression A low-weather pressure system that brings changeable weather, often rain, cloud and wind.

Destination The place that someone is travelling to.

Development aid Aid that is given to help a country to improve its living standards so that it can progress.

Diet The usual food that people eat.

Donor A country that gives aid to another country.

Dormant volcano A volcano that is not active now but may erupt again.

Drainage basin The area of land drained by a river.

Earthquake Shaking and vibration of the ground caused by movements of the Earth's crust.

Economic asset Something or somebody that makes money for a family or a country, for example, children in LEDCs who work to boost their family's income.

Economic burden Something or somebody that costs a family or a country money, for example, children who are too young to work.

Emergency relief aid Aid that is given to help solve the problems caused by a disaster such as an earthquake or flooding.

Emigration The movement of people out of a country.

Enquiry Geographers carry out an enquiry or investigation to find out about people and places.

Epicentre The point on the ground above the focus of an earthquake where the vibration is greatest.

Equator An imaginary line round the middle of the Earth which represents the 00° line of latitude.

Eruption When a volcano erupts, magma from inside the Earth escapes to the surface.

Evacuate   Take people from a place that is dangerous because of, for example, floods or an earthquake, to a safer place.

Evaluation   Looking at something to see how well done or useful it is by looking at its strengths and weaknesses.

Evaporate   Change from a liquid into a gas, for example from water into water vapour.

Extinct volcano   A volcano that is unlikely to erupt again in the future.

Factor   One of the reasons for something.

Favela   Brazilian for shanty town.

Focus   The focus of an earthquake is the point under the ground that the shock waves travel out from.

Front   When warm and cold air masses meet, the boundary is called a front.

Geothermal energy   Heat energy from the Earth that can be used to generate electricity.

Global warming   The slow increase in world temperatures due to pollution in the atmosphere.

Groundwater   The water that flows beneath the ground surface.

Hypothesis   A theory about something that can be tested by an enquiry.

Immigration   The movement of people into a country.

Impermeable   A surface that does not allow liquid to pass through it.

Infant mortality rate   The number of babies who die before they reach their first birthday for every 1000 babies born.

Infiltrate   When a liquid sinks in through a permeable surface.

Informal work   Work which does not have a regular wage, and where the worker does not pay taxes.

In-migration   The movement of people into a place.

Inoculate   To protect someone from a disease by giving them a pill or injection containing a minute amount of the organism that causes it.

Irrigate   To transport water to an area where there is a shortage, usually for growing crops.

Labour   The workforce of a country or place.

Lahar   A mud-flow made of a mixture of volcanic ash and water.

Lava   Liquid rock that flows down the sides of a volcano.

Less Economically Developed Country (LEDC)   A country with a poor economy where many people live in rural areas.

Life expectancy   The average number of years that a person might expect to live. This varies from country to country, depending on diet, health care, etc.

Linear   A pattern that forms in a straight line.

Lines of latitude   Imaginary lines drawn around the Earth from east to west parallel to the Equator.

Lines of longitude   Imaginary lines drawn around the Earth from north to south and going through both Poles.

Location   The position of a place or other feature.

Magma   Molten rock from beneath the surface of the Earth that escapes to the surface when a volcano erupts. It appears as liquid lava, volcanic bombs, ash, dust, steam and gases.

Magnitude   How large or important something is.

Mantle   The layer of hot, molten rock that comes between the Earth's crust and its core.

Migration   The movement of people from one place to another.

Minutes   Latitude and longitude are measured in degrees and minutes. There are 60 minutes in a degree.

Monitoring   Making measurements at regular intervals to see if there are any changes. In earthquake areas, for example, scientists use seismographs to detect the first signs of ground movement.

More Economically Developed Country (MEDC)   A country with a wealthy economy where a high percentage of people live in urban areas.

Multinational   Multinational companies do business all over the world.

North–South Development Line   An imaginary line that separates the richer countries (MEDCs) of the north and Oceania from the poorer countries (LEDCs) of South America, Asia and Africa.

Official aid   Aid that is given by a government and paid for by its taxpayers.

Out-migration   The movement of people out of a place.

Perception   Viewpoint; somebody's opinion.

Permanent settlement   A place where people live throughout the year, such as a housing estate.

Permeable   A surface that allows liquid to pass through it.

Population density   The number of people per area of land. This is **high** when many people live in a place, or **low** where only a few people live.

Population pyramid   A type of bar chart that shows the population structure of a country. Because the number of babies goes at the bottom of the chart and the number of very old people at the top, the chart often looks like a pyramid.

Population structure   The age groups that make up the population of a country.

Precipitation   Water falling from the air to Earth as rain, hail, sleet or snow.

Prediction   Estimating what is going to happen in the future.

Primary data   Information that you find out for yourself by looking, counting or asking people questions.

Prime Meridian   The line 0 ° of longitude that passes through Greenwich, near London.

Process of thinking   The learning process can be broken into four stages: cueing, acting, monitoring and verifying.

Recipient   A country that receives aid from another country.

Relief   The shape of an area of land – whether it is flat, hilly or mountainous.

Richter Scale   The magnitude of an earthquake can be described using the Richter Scale. Each point on the scale is ten times bigger than the one below it. An earthquake measuring 7 on the Richter Scale is ten times stronger than one measuring 6.

Sanitation   Keeping places clean and hygienic, usually by a sewage system and a supply of clean water.

Satellite image   A photograph of part of the Earth's surface taken from a satellite in space.

Secondary data   Information that you get from maps, books, CD-ROMs or the Internet.

Seismograph   An instrument that measures the shaking of the ground to give the magnitude of an earthquake. It records the vibrations on a graph called a seismogram.

Self-build housing   Houses built by the people who are going to live in them, for example in shanty towns.

Settlement   A place where people live. It may be just a few homes or a large city.

Shanty town   A squatter settlement, often on the outskirts of a city, built by people on land that does not belong to them.

Shock waves   Shock waves travel out from the focus of an earthquake into the surrounding area, making the ground vibrate.

Site   The exact location of a settlement. This often includes the physical features of the place it is built on, such as whether it is by a river.

Situation The broader picture of where a place is. A settlement's situation can be described by looking at an atlas.

Sparsely populated An area with a low population density, i.e. few people live there.

Stable population A population that is not getting larger or smaller because the death rate and the birth rate are the same.

Surface run-off The flow of water over the ground surface, including rivers and streams.

Symbol A sign or emblem that is used to represent something, such as a symbol on a map. A map has a key to show what each symbol means.

Synoptic chart A map that shows the areas of high and low pressure in a region at a particular time.

Tectonic plates The Earth's crust is made up of huge slabs called tectonic plates.

Temperate A climate, like that of the British Isles, that is neither very hot nor very cold is temperate.

Temporary settlement A place where people live for a short time, such as a nomad encampment or an oil rig.

Thematic A thematic map shows how a feature varies across a country, such as rainfall or population density.

Transnational A transnational company does business all over the world.

Transpire Leafy plants take water in through their roots and transpire it into the air as water vapour through pores in their leaves.

Tributary A river that flows into a larger river.

UNICEF United Nations Children's Fund.

Vegetation The plants in a particular area.

Venn diagram A diagram used to show the relationships within a set of items.

Vent The opening in a volcano where molten rock escapes to the surface.

Volcanic bombs Lumps of molten rock that solidify as they fall from the sky during a volcanic eruption.

Volcano An opening in the Earth's crust where molten rock from inside the Earth is able to escape to the surface.

Voluntary aid Aid that is given by individuals through charities such as the Red Cross.

Water cycle A continuous process in which water falls to Earth from the air as precipitation, evaporates and condenses to form clouds, and falls back to Earth again.

Weather The conditions of the atmosphere, such as the temperature, amount of rain or hours of sunshine.

Weather system An anticyclone or a depression.

Index

active zones 24, 30, 42
aid 20, 40–1, 86
Angeles City (Philippines) 29
annotated sketches 5
annual growth rate of
    population 46
Antarctica 56
anticyclones 96
Aston Villa 108–10, 113
atlases 6–7, 68

Barra da Tijuca (Brazil) 71–2
Birmingham 93
birth rates 46, 48
Bridgnorth 61, 63
British Isles 90, 91, 94–7

Central Business Districts
    (CBDs) 70, 73
charities 40, 41, 86
cities 68–73
condensation 76
crust 30, 34

data 12, 14, 19
death rates 46, 47
decision–making 108–13
depressions 96–7
development compass roses 110
distances, measuring on a map 13
dot maps 15
drainage basins 78–9

Earth 8, 30
earthquakes 20–4, 30–9, 40–1, 43
England 88–99
enquiries 10–19, 101
Equator 8
evaporation 76

fast food restaurants 10–17
favelas 71, 72, 73
flow charts 18
football 102–7, 114
football grounds 108–13
flooding 74–5, 77–87
fronts 96

GDP (Gross Domestic
    Product) 114
geographical questions 5, 10, 12,
    19, 75
graphs 106, 107
Great Britain 90
Gross Domestic Product
    (GDP) 114
groundwater 76

Hong Kong 52

images 88, 92–3, 99
impermeable ground 76–7
infant mortality rates 46, 48
infiltration 76–7, 79
investigations 10–19, 101
Izmit earthquake (Turkey, 1999)
    30, 31, 34–7, 41

lahars (mudflows) 28, 29
latitude 6, 8
LEDCs (Less Economically Developed
    Countries) 16, 46, 47, 48, 87, 114
life expectancy 46
Llanidloes 61, 64
longitude 6, 8

magma 25
Mali 46, 48, 49, 51, 52, 54–5
Manchester United 102–3
maps, measuring distances 13
McDonald's restaurants 14–16
MEDCs (More Economically
    Developed Countries) 16, 46, 47,
    48, 87
migration 46, 72
mind maps 87
More Economically Developed
Countries (MEDCs) 16, 46, 47,
    48, 87
Mount Pinatubo (Philippines)
    25, 26–9
Mozambique 74–5, 84–6, 87
multinational corporations
    16, 101

North–South Development
    Line 16, 114

Oxford United 111–13

perceptions 88–9, 92, 98, 99
permeable ground 76–7
Philippines 25, 26–9
plates, tectonic 24, 30
population 44–6, 50–7, 91
population density 52–3, 57
population distribution 15, 54–7
population pyramids 51
population structure 50–1
precipitation 76, 78, 84
primary data 12

questionnaires 12
questions, geographical 5, 10, 12,
    19, 75

restaurants, fast food 10–17
Richter scale 30, 31, 34
Rio de Janeiro (Brazil) 68–73
River Severn 61–7, 78–81
rivers, flooding 75, 78–83, 84
Rocinha (Brazil) 71
routes 104–5
run–off 76–7, 79

satellite photographs 6, 8, 29, 97
scattergraphs 95
secondary data 12, 13
seismographs 30, 38
settlements 58–67, 68
Severn, River 61–7, 78–81
shanty towns 71, 72, 73
Shrewsbury 78, 79, 80–1
sites of settlements 60–7, 68,
    70, 73
situations of settlements 68, 73
sketches 5
sport 100–1, 115
surface run–off 76–7, 79
synoptic charts 96

tectonic plates 24, 30
Tewkesbury 61, 62
time lines 18
tourism 29, 98
transnational companies 16, 101
transpiration 76, 79
transport 104–5
Turkish earthquake (Izmit, 1999)
    30, 31, 34–7, 41

UK (United Kingdom) 90
flooding 75, 78–83, 86, 87
population 46, 48–9, 51, 52
UNICEF (United Nations Children's
    Fund) 41

Venn diagrams 86, 90
volcanic eruptions 25, 26–9, 40
volcanoes 20–4, 25–9, 43

water cycle 76–7
wealth 114
weather, British Isles 94–7, 98
Welshpool 61, 65
Worcester 61, 66
wordscapes 25